CRAFTSMAN HOMES

Jeff,
I can't wait to build
a home with you.
All my love,
Karen

CRAFTSMAN HOMES
BY GUSTAV STICKLEY

THE LYONS PRESS

Guilford, Connecticut

An imprint of The Globe Pequot Press

First Lyons Press edition, 2002

The Lyons Press is an imprint of The Globe Pequot Press.

Originally published in 1909 by The Craftsman Publishing Company

Printed in the United States of America

2 4 6 8 10 9 7 5 3 1

Library of Congress Cataloging-in-Publication Data is available on file.

ISBN 1-58574-492-1

"Great nations write their autobiography in three manuscripts: the book of their words, the book of their deeds and the book of their art. Not one of these books can be understood unless we read the other two, but of the three, the only one quite trustworthy is the last. The acts of a nation may be triumphant by its good fortune, and its words mighty by the genius of a few of its children, but its art can be supreme only by the general gifts and common sympathies of the race."

John Ruskin.

TABLE OF CONTENTS

TABLE OF CONTENTS—*Continued*

"Beauty does not consist so much in the things represented, as in the need one has had of expressing them; and this need it is which creates the degree of force with which one acquits oneself of the work. One may say that everything is beautiful provided the thing turns up in its own proper time and in its own place; and contrariwise that nothing can be beautiful arriving inappropriately."

Jean François Millet.

"THE SIMPLIFICATION OF LIFE:" A CHAPTER FROM EDWARD CARPENTER'S BOOK CALLED "ENGLAND'S IDEAL"

WHEN we remember the sincere reformers of the world, do we not always recall most gladly the simple men amongst them, Savonarola rather than Tolstoi, Gorky rather than Goethe, and would it not be difficult to associate this memory of individual effort for public good with consciously elegant surroundings. Could we, for instance, picture Savonarola with a life handicapped, perhaps, by eager pursuit of sartorial eccentricities, with a bias for elaborate cuisine and insistence upon unearned opulence, or the earning of luxury at the sacrifice of other's lives or happiness? It does not somehow fit into the frame. In remembering those who have dedicated their lives to the benefit of their own lands, we inevitably picture them as men of simple ways, who have asked little and given much, who have freed their shoulders from the burdens of luxury, who have stripped off from their lives the tight inflexible bandages of unnecessary formalities, and who have thus been left free for those great essentials of honest existence, for courage, for unselfishness, for heroic purpose and, above all, for the clear vision which means the acceptance of that final good, honesty of purpose, without which there can be no real meaning in life.

Such right living and clear thinking cannot find abiding place except among those whose lives bring them back close to Nature's ways, those who are content to be clad simply and comfortably, to accept from life only just compensation for useful toil, who prefer to live much in the open, finding in the opportunity for labor the right to live; those who desire to rest from toil in homes built to meet their individual need of rest and peace and joy, homes which realize a personal standard of comfort and beauty; those who demand honesty in all expression from all friends, and who give in return sincerity and unselfishness, those who are fearless of sorrow, yet demand joy; those who rank work and rest as equal means of progress—in such lives only may we find the true regeneration for any nation, for only in such simplicity and sincerity can a nation develop a condition of permanent and properly equalized welfare.

By simplicity here is not meant any foolish whimsical eccentricity of dress or manner or architecture, colonized and made conspicuous by useless wealth, for eccentricity is but an expression of individual egotism and as such must inevitably be short-lived. And what our formal, artificial world of today needs is not more of this sort of eccentricity and egotism, but less; not more conscious posing for picturesque reform, but greater and quieter achievement along lines of fearless honesty; not less beauty, but infinitely more of a beauty that is real and lasting because it is born out of use and taste.

From generation to generation every nation has the privilege of nourishing men and women (but a few) who think and live thus sincerely and beautifully, and who so far as possible strive to impress upon their own generation the need of such sincerity and beauty in daily life. One of the rarest and most honest of these sincere personalities in modern life is Edward Carpenter, an Englishman who, though born to wealth and station, has stripped his life of superfluous social paraphernalia and stepped out of the clumsy burden of tradition, up (not down) to the life of the simple, common people, earning his living and that of his family as a cobbler (and a good one, too) and living in a peaceful fashion in a home planned and largely constructed by himself. His life and his work are with the people. He knows their point of view, he writes for them, lectures for them, and though a leader in modern thought in England and a man of genius, he is one with his daily associates in purpose and general scheme of existence. In all his present writings the common man and his relation to civilization, is Mr. Carpenter's theme, and he deals with the great problems of sociology in plain practical terms and with a straightforward thought born of that surest knowledge possible, experience.

From the beginning of the endeavor of THE CRAFTSMAN to aid in the interests of better art, better work and a better and more reasonable way of living, the work of Edward Carpenter has been an inspiration and an ideal, born out of that sympathy of purpose which makes men of whatever nation brothers and comrades. We have from time to time in the magazine quoted from Mr. Carpenter's books at length, feeling that he was expressing our own ideal as no words of ours could, and particularly have we felt a oneness of purpose with him in his book called "England's Ideal," in which he publishes a chapter on the "Simplification of Life," which with its honesty, sincerity, its high courage and rare judgment should make clear the pathway for all of those among us who are honestly interested in readjusting life on a plane of greater usefulness and higher beauty. In this essay which we purpose here to quote at length, Mr. Carpenter begins by speaking of his own method of readjusting his life as follows:

"IF YOU do not want to be a vampire and a parasite upon others, the great question of practical life which everyone has to face, is how to carry it on with as little labor and effort as may be. No one wants to labor needlessly, and if you have to earn everything you spend, economy becomes a very personal question—not necessarily in the pinching sense, but merely as adaptation of means to the end. When I came some years ago to live with cottagers (earning say £50 to £60 a year) and share their life, I was surprised to find how little both in labor and expense their food cost them, who were doing far more work than I was, or indeed the generality of the people among whom I had been living. This led me to see that the somewhat luxurious mode of living I had been accustomed to was a mere waste, as far as adaptation to any useful end was concerned; and afterward I had decided that it had been a positive hindrance, for when I became habituated to a more simple life and diet, I found that a marked improvement took place in my powers both of mind and body.

"The difference arising from having a small piece of garden is very great, and makes one feel how important it is that every cottage should have a plot of ground attached. A rood of land (quarter acre) is sufficient to grow all potatoes and other vegetables and some fruit for the year's use, say for a family of five. Half an acre would be an ample allowance. Such a piece of land may easily be cultivated by anyone in the odd hours of regular work, and the saving is naturally large from not having to go to the shop for everything of this nature that is needed.

"Of course, the current mode of life is so greatly wasteful, and we have come to consider so many things as necessaries—whether in food, furniture, clothing or what not—which really bring us back next to no profit or pleasure compared with the labor spent upon them, that it is really difficult to know where the balance of true economy would stand if, so to speak, left to itself. All we can do is to take the existing mode of life in its simpler forms, somewhat as above, and work from that as a basis. For though the cottager's way of living, say in our rural districts or in the neighborhood of our large towns, is certainly superior to that of the well-to-do, that does not argue that it is not capable of improvement. * * * *

"NO DOUBT immense simplifications of our daily life are possible; but this does not seem to be a matter which has been much studied. Rather hitherto the tendency has been all the other way, and every additional ornament to the mantelpiece has been regarded as an acquisition and not as a nuisance; though one doesn't see any reason, in the nature of things, why it should be regarded as one more than the other. It cannot be too often remembered that every additional object in a house requires additional dusting, cleaning, repairing; and lucky you are if its requirements stop there. When you abandon a wholesome tile or stone floor for a Turkey carpet, you are setting out on a voyage of which you cannot see the end. The Turkey carpet makes the old furniture look uncomfortable, and calls for stuffed couches and armchairs; the couches and armchairs demand a walnut-wood table; the walnut-wood table requires polishing, and the polish bottles require shelves; the couches and armchairs have casters and springs, which give way and want mending; they have damask seats, which fade and must be covered; the chintz covers require washing, and when washed they call for antimacassars to keep them clean. The antimacassars require wool, and the wool requires knitting-needles, and the knitting-needles require a box, the box demands a side table to stand on and the side table involves more covers and casters—and so we go on. Meanwhile the carpet wears out and has to be supplemented by bits of drugget, or eked out with oilcloth, and beside the daily toil required to keep this mass of rubbish in order, we have every week or month, instead of the pleasant cleaning-day of old times, a terrible domestic convulsion and bouleversement of the household.

"It is said by those who have traveled in Arabia that the reason why there are so many religious enthusiasts in that country, is that in the extreme simplicity of the life and uniformity of the landscape there, heaven—in the form of the intense blue sky—seems close upon one. One may almost see God. But we moderns guard ourselves effectually against this danger. For beside the smoke pall which covers our towns, we raise in each household such a dust of trivialities that our attention is fairly absorbed, and if this screen subsides for a moment we are sure to have the daily paper up before our eyes so that if a chariot of fire were sent to fetch us, ten to one we should not see it.

"However, if this multiplying of the complexity of life is really grateful to some people, one cannot quarrel with them for pursuing it; and to many it appears to be so. When a sewing machine is introduced into a household the simple-minded husband thinks that, as it works ten times as quick as the hand, there will now be only a tenth part of the time spent by his wife and daughter in sewing that there was before. But he is ignorant of human nature. To his surprise he finds that there is no difference in the time. The difference is in the plaits and flounces—they put ten times as many on their dresses. Thus we see how little external reforms avail. If the desire for simplicity is not really present, no labor-saving appliances will make life simpler.

"As a rule all curtains, hangings, cloths and covers, which are not absolutely necessary, would be dispensed with. They all create dust and stiffness, and all entail trouble and recurring expense, and they all tempt the housekeeper to keep out the air and sunlight—two things of the last and most vital importance. I like a room which looks its best when the sun streams into it through wide open doors and windows. If the furnishing of it cannot stand this test—if it looks uncomfortable under the operation—you may be sure there is something unwholesome about it. As to the question of elegance or adornment, that may safely be left to itself. The studied effort to make interiors elegant has only ended—in what we see. After all, if things are in their places they will always look well. What, by common consent, is more graceful than a ship—the sails, the spars, the rigging, the lines of the hull? Yet go on board and you will scarcely find one thing placed there for the purpose of adornment. An imperious necessity rules everything; this rope could have no other place than it has, nor could be less thick or thicker than it is; and it is, in fact, this necessity which makes the ship beautiful. * * * *

"WITH regard to clothing, as with furniture and the other things, it can be much simplified if one only desires it so. Probably, however, most people do not desire it, and of course they are right in keeping to the complications. Who knows but what there is some influence at work for some ulterior purpose which we do not guess, in causing us to artificialize our lives to the extraordinary extent we do in modern times? Our ancestors wore woad, and it does not at first sight seem obvious why we should not do the same. Without, however, entering into the woad question, we may consider some ways in which clothing may be simplified without departing far from the existing standard. It seems to be generally admitted now that wool is the most suitable material as a rule. I find that a good woolen coat, such as is ordinarily worn, feels warmer when unlined than it does when a layer of silk or cotton is interposed between the woolen surface and the body. It is also lighter; thus in both ways the simplification is a gain. Another advantage is that it washes easier and better, and is at all times cleaner. No one who has had the curiosity to unpick the lining of a tailor-made coat that has been in wear a little time, will, I think, ever wish to have coats made on the same principle again. The rubbish he will find inside, the frettings and frayings of the cloth collected in little dirt-heaps up and down, the paddings of cotton wool, the odd lots of miscellaneous stuff used as backings, the quantity of canvas stiffening, the tags and paraphernalia connected with the pockets, bits of buckram inserted here and there to make the coat "sit" well—all these things will be a warning to him. * * * *

"And certainly, nowadays, many folk visibly are in their coffins. Only the head and hands are out, all the rest of the body clearly sickly with want of light and air, atrophied, stiff in the joints, strait-waistcoated, and partially mummied. Sometimes it seems to me that is the reason why, in our modern times, the curious intellect is so abnormally developed, the brain and the tongue waggle so, because these organs alone have a chance, the rest are shut out from heaven's light and air; the poor human heart grown feeble and weary in its isolation and imprisonment, the liver diseased and the lungs strait-ened down to mere sighs and conventional disconsolate sounds beneath their cerements.

"There are many other ways in which the details and labor of daily life may be advantageously reduced, which will occur to anyone who turns practical attention to the matter. For myself I confess to a great pleasure in witnessing the Economics of Life—and how seemingly nothing need be wasted; how the very stones that offend the spade in the garden become invaluable when foot-paths have to be laid out or drains to be made. Hats that are past wear get cut up into strips for nailing creepers on the wall; the upper leathers of old shoes are useful for the same purpose. The under garment that is too far gone for mending is used for patching another less decrepit of its kind, then it is torn up into strips for bandages or what not; and when it has served its time thus it de-scends to floor washing, and is scrubbed out of life—useful to the end. When my coat has worn itself into an affectionate intimacy with my body, when it has served for Sunday best, and for week days, and got weather-stained out in the fields with the sun and rain—then faithful, it does not part from me, but getting it-self cut up into shreds and patches descends to form a hearthrug for my feet. After that, when worn through, it goes into the kennel and keeps my dog warm, and so after lapse of years, retiring to the manure-heaps and passing out on to the land, returns to me in the form of potatoes for my dinner; or being pastured by my sheep, reappears upon their backs as the material of new clothing. Thus it remains a friend to all time, grateful to me for not having despised and thrown it away when it first got behind the fashions. And seeing we have been faithful to each other, my coat and I, for one round or life-period, I do not see why we should not renew our intimacy—in other metamorphoses—or why we should ever quite lose touch of each other through the æons.

"In the above sketch my object has been not so much to put forward any theory of the conduct of daily life, or to maintain that one method of living is of itself superior to another, as to try and come at the facts connected with the sub-ject. In the long run every household has to support itself; the benefits and accommodations it receives from society have to be covered by the labor it ex-pends for society. This cannot be got over. The present effort of a large number of people to live on interest and dividends, and so in a variety of ways on the labor of others, is simply an effort to make water run up hill; it cannot last very long. The balance, then, between the labor that you may consume and the labor that you expend may be struck in many different ways, but it has to be struck; and I have been interested to bring together some materials for an easy solution of the problem."

"THE ART OF BUILDING A HOME": BY BARRY PARKER AND RAYMOND UNWIN

S A nation we do not easily submit to coercion. We want a hand in the government, national or local. We are pretty direct if we do not like a senator or a governor, and express our opinion fully of our ministers and college presidents. In more intimate matters of courtship and marriage we regard ourselves as more independent than any other nation. We marry usually whom we please, and live where we please, and work as we please—but when it comes to that most vital matter—building a home, individuality and independence seem to vanish, and we are browbeaten alike by architect, builder, contractor, interior decorator, picture dealer and furniture man. We live in any old house that anyone else has discarded, and we submit to all manner of tyrannies as to the size, style and finish of our houses, impertinences that we would not permit in any other detail of life. We not only imitate foreign ideals in our architecture, but we have become artificial and unreal in all the detail of the finish and fittings of our homes. How many of us would dare to rise up and assert sufficient individuality to plan and build a house that exactly suited our personal ideal of comfort and beauty, and represented our station in life?

And to what extent can we hope for finer ideals in a country that is afraid to be sincere in that most significant feature of national achievement—the home. We are a country of self-supporting men and women, and we cannot expect to develop an honest significant architecture until we build homes that are simple, yet beautiful, that proclaim fine democratic standards and that are essentially appropriate to busy intelligent people.

That this same state of affairs prevails somewhat in other lands (though nowhere to the same extent as in America) we realize from the writing of two well-known English architects, Barry Parker and Raymond Unwin, who in a series of lectures published under the title of "The Art of Building a Home" have entered a plea for greater honesty in architecture and greater sincerity in decoration which ought to strike a responsive chord in the heart of every American who has contemplated the foolish, unthinking, artificial structures which we have vainly called homes.

In the introduction to this vital valuable little book Messrs. Parker and Unwin take up the question of lack of thought in architecture in so simple, straightforward and illuminating a fashion that it has seemed wise to present it to the readers of CRAFTSMAN HOMES as expressing our creeds and establishing more fully our own ideals!

"THE way we run in ruts is wonderful: our inability to find out the right principles upon which to set to work to accomplish what we take in hand, or to go to the bottom of things, is simply astonishing: while the resignation with which we accept the Recognized and Usual as the Right and Inevitable is really beautiful.

"In nothing is this tendency more noticeable than in the art of house-building. We begin by considering what, in the way of a house, our neighbors have; what they would expect us to have; what is customary in the rank of life to which we belong; anything, in fact, but what are our actual needs. About the last thing

6

THE ART OF BUILDING A HOME

we do is to make our home take just that form which will, in the most straight-forward manner, meet our requirements. * * * *

"The planning having been dictated by convention, all the details are worked out under the same influence. To each house is applied a certain amount of meaningless mechanical and superficial ornamentation according to some recognized standard. No use whatever is made of the decorative properties inherent in the construction and in the details necessary to the building. These are put as far as possible out of sight. For example, latches and locks are all let into the doors leaving visible the knobs only. The hinges are hidden in the rebate of the door frame, while the real door frame, that which does the work, is covered up with a strip of flimsy molded board styled the architrave. All constructional features, wherever possible, are smeared over with a coat of plaster to bring them up to the same dead level of flat monotony, leaving a clear field for the erection of the customary abominations in the form of cornices, imitation beams where no beams are wanted, and plaster brackets which could support, and do support, nothing. Even with the fire the chief aim seems to be to acknowledge as few of its properties and characteristics as possible; it is buried as deep in the wall and as far out of sight and out of the way as may be; it is smothered up with as much uncongenial and inappropriate "enrichment" as can be crowded round it; and, to add the final touch of senseless incongruity, some form of that massive and *apparently* very constructional and essential thing we call a mantelpiece is erected, in wood, stone or marble, towering it may be even to the ceiling. If we were not so accustomed to it, great would be our astonishment to find that this most prominent feature has really no function whatever, beyond giving cause for a lot of other things as useful and beautiful as itself, which exist only that they may be put upon it, 'to decorate it.' * * * *

"The essence and life of design lies in finding that form for anything which will, with the maximum of convenience and beauty, fit it for the particular functions it has to perform, and adapt it to the special circumstances in which it must be placed. Perhaps the most fruitful source whence charm of design arises in anything, is the grace with which it serves its purpose and conforms to its surroundings. How many of the beautiful features of the work of past ages, which we now arbitrarily reproduce and copy, arose out of the skilful and graceful way in which some old artist-craftsman, or chief mason, got over a difficulty! If, instead of copying these features when and where the cause for them does not exist, we would rather emulate the spirit in which they were produced, there would be more hope of again seeing life and vigor in our architecture and design.

"WHEN the architect leaves the house, the subservience to convention is not over. After him follow the decorator and the furnisher, who try to overcome the lifelessness and vapidity by covering all surfaces with fugitive decorations and incongruous patterns, and filling the rooms with flimsy stereotyped furniture and nick-nacks. To these the mistress of the house will be incessantly adding, from an instinctive feeling of the incompleteness and unsatisfactoriness of the whole. Incidentally we see here one reason why the influence of the architect should not stop at the completion of the four walls, but should extend to the last detail of the furnished house. When his responsibility ceases with the erection of the shell, it is natural that he should look very little beyond this. There is no inducement for him to work out any definite scheme for a finished room, for he knows that if he had any aim the decorator and furnisher would certainly miss it and would fail to complete his creation. If, when designing a house, the architect were bearing in mind the effect each room would have when finished and furnished, his conceptions would be influenced from the very beginning, and his attitude toward the work would tend to undergo an entire change. At present he but too readily accepts the popular idea of art as a thing quite apart from life, a sort of trimming to be added if funds allow.

"It is this prevalent conception of beauty as a sweetmeat, something rather nice which may be taken or left according to inclination after the solid meal has been secured, which largely causes the lack of comeliness we find in our houses. Before this idea can be dispelled and we can appreciate either the place which art should hold in our lives or the importance of rightly educating the appreciation of it, we must realize that beauty is part of the necessary food of any life worth the name; that art, which is the expression of beauty as conceived and created by man, is primarily concerned with the making of the useful garments of life beautiful, not with the trimming of them; and that, moreover, in its higher branches art is the medium through which the most subtle ideas are conveyed from man to man.

"Understanding something of the true meaning of art, we may set about realizing it, at least in the homes which are so much within our control. Let us have in our houses, rooms where there shall be space to carry on the business of life freely and with pleasure, with furniture made for use; rooms where a drop of water spilled is not fatal; where the life of a child is not made a burden to it by unnecessary restraint; plain, simple, and ungarnished if necessary, but honest. Let us have such ornament as we do have really beautiful and wrought by hand, carving, wrought metal, embroidery, painting, something which it has given pleasure to the producer to create, and which shows this in every line—the only possible work of art. Let us call in the artist, bid him leave his easel pictures, and paint on our walls and over the chimney corner landscapes and scenes which shall bring light and life into the room; which shall speak of nature, purity, and truth; shall become part of the room, of the walls on which they are painted, and of the lives of us who live beside them; paintings which our children shall grow up to love, and always connect with scenes of home with that vividness of a memory from childhood which no time can efface. Then, if necessary, let the rest of the walls go untouched in all the rich variety of color and tone, of light and shade, of the naked brickwork. Let the floor go uncarpeted, and the wood unpainted, that we may have time to think, and money with which to educate our children to think also. Let us have rooms which once decorated are always decorated, rooms fit to be homes in the fullest poetry of the name; in which no artificiality need momentarily force us to feel shame for things of which we know there is nothing to be ashamed: rooms which can form backgrounds, fitting and dignified, at the time and in our memories, for all those little scenes, those acts of kindness and small duties, as well as the scenes of deep emotion and trial, which make up the drama of our lives at home."

A CRAFTSMAN HOUSE FOUNDED ON THE CALIFORNIA MISSION STYLE

E have selected for presentation here what we consider the best of the houses designed in The Craftsman Workshops and published in THE CRAFTSMAN during the past five years. Brought together in this way into a closely related group, these designs serve to show the development of the Craftsman idea of home building, decoration and furnishing, and to make plain the fundamental principles which underlie the planning of every Craftsman house. These principles are simplicity, durability, fitness for the life that is to be lived in the house and harmony with its natural surroundings. Given these things, the beauty and comfort of the home environment develops as naturally as a flowering plant from the root.

As will be seen, these houses range from the simplest little cottages or bungalows costing only a few hundred dollars, up to large and expensive residences. But they are all Craftsman houses, nevertheless, and all are designed with regard to the kind of durability that will insure freedom from the necessity of frequent repairs; to the greatest economy of space and material, and to the securing of plenty of space and freedom in the interior of the house by doing away with unnecessary partitions and the avoidance of any kind of crowding. For interest, beauty, and the effect of home comfort and welcome, we depend upon the liberal use of wood finished in such a way that all its friendliness is revealed; upon warmth, richness, and variety in the color scheme of walls, rugs and draperies, and upon the charm of structural features such as chimneypieces,

window-seats, staircases, fireside nooks, and built-in furnishings of all kinds, our object being to have each room so interesting in itself that it seems complete before a single piece of furniture is put into it.

This plain cement house has been selected for presentation at the head of the list chiefly because it was the first house designed in The Craftsman Workshops and was published in THE CRAFTSMAN for January, 1904, for the benefit of the newly formed Home Builders' Club. Therefore it serves to furnish us with a starting point from which we may judge whether or not any advance has since been made in the application of the Craftsman idea to the planning and furnishing of houses.

It was only natural that our first expression of this idea should take shape in a house which, without being exactly founded on the Mission architecture so much used in California, is nevertheless reminiscent of that style, this effect being given by the low broad proportions of the building and the use of shallow, round arches over the entrance and the two openings which give light and air to the recessed porch in front. The thick cement walls are left rough, a primitive treatment that produces a quality and texture difficult to obtain by any other method and to which time and weather lend additional interest. The roof, which is low pitched and has a fairly strong projection, is covered with unglazed red Spanish tile in the usual lap-roll pattern with ridge rolls and cresting. The house, as it stands, is a fair example of the way in which the problem of the exterior has been solved by the combination of three factors: simplicity of building materials, employment of constructive features as the only

Published in The Craftsman, January, 1904

A CRAFTSMAN HOUSE BUILT OF CEMENT OR CONCRETE AFTER THE CALIFORNIA MISSION STYLE, WITH LOW-PITCHED TILED ROOF, ROUND ARCHES AND STRAIGHT MASSIVE WALLS. THE DECORATIVE EFFECT DEPENDS ENTIRELY UPON COLOR, PROPORTIONS AND STRUCTURAL FEATURES.

A CRAFTSMAN HOUSE IN CALIFORNIA MISSION STYLE

decoration, and the recognition of the color element which is so necessary in bringing about the necessary harmony between the house and its surroundings. In this case the walls are

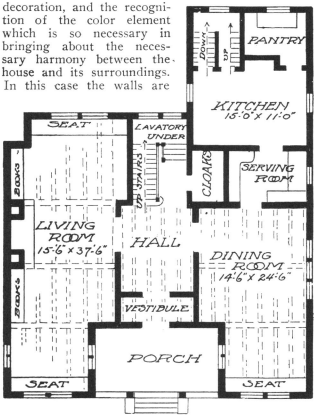

FIRST STORY FLOOR PLAN.

treated with a pigment that gives a soft warm creamy tone, almost a biscuit color, and the roof is dull red,—a scheme that is excellently suited to the prevailing color in California or in the South, where yellows, browns and violets abound. For the colder coloring of the northern or eastern landscape, the cement walls might either be left in the natural gray, or given a tone of dull green, which, applied unevenly, gives an admirable effect upon rough cast plaster. Or, for that matter, the house might be built of brick, stone, or of any one of the various forms of concrete construction. And the roof could be of tile, heavy shingles, or, if given a steeper pitch, of heavy, rough slate. In fact, the design as shown here is chiefly suggestive in its nature, making clear the fundamental principles of the Craftsman house and leaving room for such variation of detail as the owner may desire.

It will be noted that the foundation is not visible and that the turf and shrubbery around it appear to cling to the walls of the house,—a circumstance that is apparently slight and yet has a good deal to do with the linking of a house to the ground on which it stands. This effect would be greatly heightened by a growth of vines over the large plain wall spaces, which would lend themselves admirably to a natural drapery of ivy or ampelopsis.

The treatment of the interior is based upon the principles already laid down, the object being to obtain the maximum effect of beauty and comfort from materials which are few in number and comparatively inexpensive. Although we have not space here for illustration of the interior features, a description of the color scheme employed and of the use made of woodwork and built-in furnishings may serve to give some idea of its character. While the outside of the house is plain to severity, the inside, as we have designed it, glows with color and is rich in suggestion of home comfort. As in all Craftsman houses, wood is abundantly used in the form of beams, wainscots and numerous built-in furnishings.

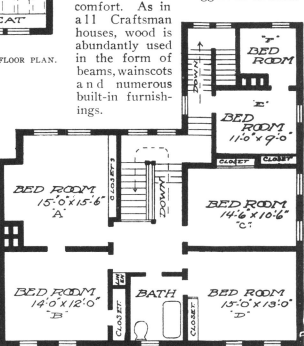

SECOND STORY FLOOR PLAN.

AN OLD-FASHIONED HOUSE WITH THE DINING ROOM AND KITCHEN IN ONE

Published in The Craftsman, May, 1905.

VIEW OF HOUSE FROM THE FRONT SHOWING DORMERS, ENTRANCE PORCH AND GROUPING OF WINDOWS.

UPON looking over the plan of this compact little dwelling, it occurs to us that possibly some people might like the general idea of the house and yet not find it convenient to go into the simple life to such an extent as to have the dining room and kitchen in one, as suggested here. Personally we like very much the homely comfort and good cheer which belongs to the big, old-fashioned kitchen which is exquisitely kept and which has in it room for the dining table. But in order to make such an arrangement a suc-

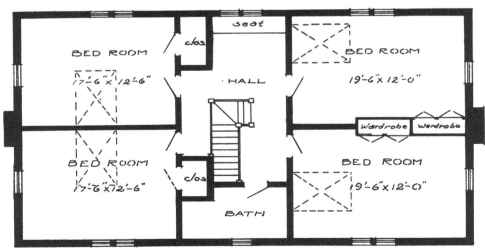

SECOND STORY FLOOR PLAN.

AN OLD-FASHIONED HOUSE

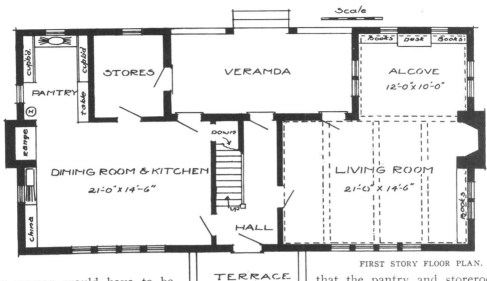

FIRST STORY FLOOR PLAN.

cess, a woman would have to be the sort of a housekeeper her grandmother probably was, and take a personal interest in her cupboard shelves and the brilliancy of her copper and brass cooking utensils, which few women nowadays have time to do.

For those who prefer a separate dining room and a kitchen proper, we would suggest that the pantry and storeroom be thrown into one and used for a kitchen. The chimney built for the range would serve equally well for a fireplace in the dining room, and the range, if set in the adjoining corner, could easily be connected with the same flue. One of the pleasantest features is the veranda at the back, which can be enclosed with glass in winter.

RECESSED VERANDA AT THE BACK OF THE HOUSE, WHICH MAY BE USED AS A DINING PORCH IN SUMMER AND GLASSED IN FOR A CONSERVATORY OR SUN ROOM IN WINTER.

AN OLD FASHIONED HOUSE

LIVING ROOM, SHOWING FIREPLACE OF SPLIT BOULDERS; NOOK WITH BUILT-IN BOOKCASES AND WRITING DESK; DIVISION OF WALL SPACES BY WAINSCOTING, STENCILED PANELS AND FRIEZE, AND EFFECT OF CASEMENTS SET HIGH IN THE WALL ABOVE THE WAINSCOT.

KITCHEN AND DINING ROOM COMBINED, SHOWING RANGE SET IN A RECESS AND HOODED TO CARRY OFF COOKING ODORS; THE DECORATIVE EFFECT OF AN OLD-FASHIONED CUPBOARD BUILT INTO THE WALL AND THE PLACING OF THE DINING TABLE BENEATH A GROUP OF FOUR WINDOWS.

A SMALL COTTAGE THAT IS COMFORTABLE, ATTRACTIVE AND INEXPENSIVE

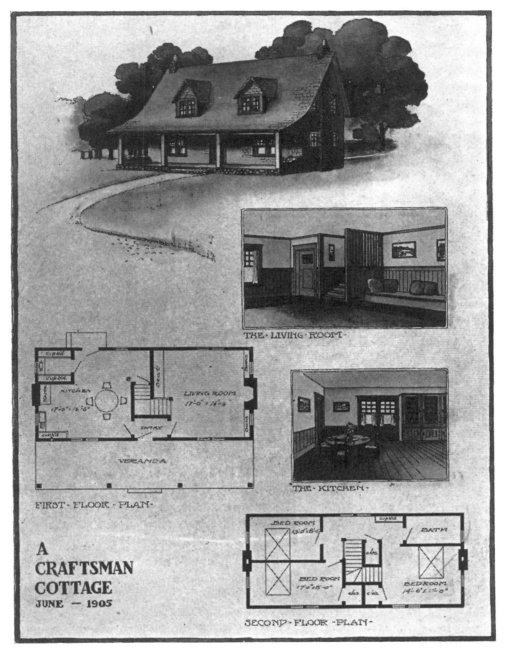

NOTE THE DIVISION OF SPACE SO THAT THE GREATEST AMOUNT OF FREEDOM AND CONVENIENCE IS OBTAINED WITHIN A SMALL AREA. THE ILLUSTRATIONS OF THE INTERIOR SERVE TO SHOW HOW THE STRUCTURAL FEATURES, ALTHOUGH SIMPLE AND INEXPENSIVE, GIVE TO EACH ROOM AN INDIVIDUAL BEAUTY AND CHARM. THE KITCHEN IS ARRANGED TO SERVE ALSO FOR A DINING ROOM.

A PLAIN HOUSE THAT WILL LAST FOR GENERATIONS AND NEED BUT FEW REPAIRS

Published in The Craftsman, July, 1905.

EXTERIOR VIEW SHOWING STRUCTURAL USE OF TIMBERS ON UPPER STORY AND EFFECT OF BUNGALOW ROOF.

MOST of the Craftsman houses are designed for an environment which admits of plenty of ground or at least of a large garden around them, but this one,—while of course at its best in such surroundings,—would serve admirably for a dwelling to be built on an ordinary city lot large enough to accommodate a house thirty feet square. Seen from the exterior, the house shows a simplicity and thoroughness of construction which makes for the greatest durability and minimizes the necessity for repairs. Also the rooms on both floors are so arranged as to utilize to the best advantage every inch of space and to afford the greatest facility for communication; a plan that tends to lighten by many degrees the burden of housekeeping.

In looking over the plan of the interior, we would suggest one modification which is more in accord with the later Craftsman houses. It will be noticed that the doors leading from the hall into the living room and dining room are of the ordinary size. We have found the feeling of space and freedom throughout the rooms intended for the common life of the family so much more attractive than the shutting off of each room into a separate compartment, so to speak, that were we to revise this plan in the light of our later experience, we would widen these openings so that the partitions would either be taken out entirely or else be suggested merely by a panel and post extending only two or three feet from the wall and open at the top after the fashion of so many of the Craftsman interiors. This device serves to break the space pleasantly by the introduction of a structural feature which is always decorative and yet to leave unhampered the space which should be clear and open.

While we advocate the utmost economy of space and urge simplicity as to furnishing, we nevertheless make it a point to render impossible even a passing impression of barrenness or monotony. As we have said, this is partly a matter of woodwork, general color scheme and interesting structural features that make each room a beautiful thing in itself, independent of any furnishing. But also we realize the never ending charm of irregularity in arrangement, that is, of having the rooms so placed and nooks and corners so abundant that the whole cannot be taken in at one glance.

In this case the simple oblong of the living room is broken by the window seat on one

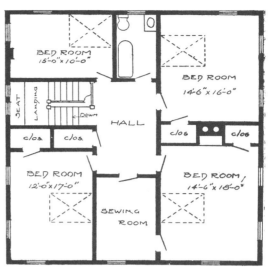

SECOND STORY FLOOR PLAN.

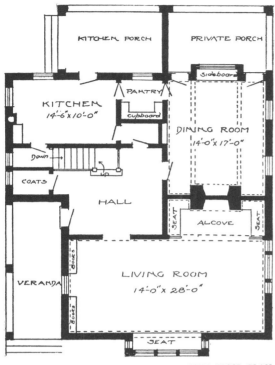

FIRST STORY FLOOR PLAN.

side and the alcove with its chimneypiece and fireside seats on the other. Just beside the alcove is a group of casement windows set high in the wall, so that the sill comes just on a level with the top of an upright piano. The same line is carried all around the room, which is wainscoted preferably with oak or chestnut.

END OF DINING ROOM, SHOWING EFFECT OF BUILT-IN SIDEBOARD, PICTURE WINDOW AND GLASS DOORS. A BUILT-IN CUPBOARD APPEARS AT THE SIDE OF THE ROOM.

A PLAIN HOUSE THAT WILL LAST FOR GENERATIONS

FIRESIDE NOOK IN THE LIVING ROOM, SHOWING ARRANGEMENT OF SEATS AND THE PLACING OF A CRAFTSMAN PIANO JUST BELOW A GROUP OF CASEMENTS. THE DECORATIONS IN THE WALL PANELS ARE STENCILED ON ROUGH PLASTER IN COLORS THAT ARE MEANT TO ACCENT THE GENERAL COLOR SCHEME.

BEDROOM SHOWING A TYPICAL CRAFTSMAN SCHEME FOR DECORATING AND FURNISHING A SLEEPING ROOM. NOTE THE DIVISION OF WALL SPACES INTO PANELS BY STRIPS OF WOOD. THE PANELS ARE COVERED WITH JAPANESE GRASS-CLOTH.

A COTTAGE OF CEMENT OR STONE THAT IS CONVENIENTLY ARRANGED FOR A SMALL FAMILY

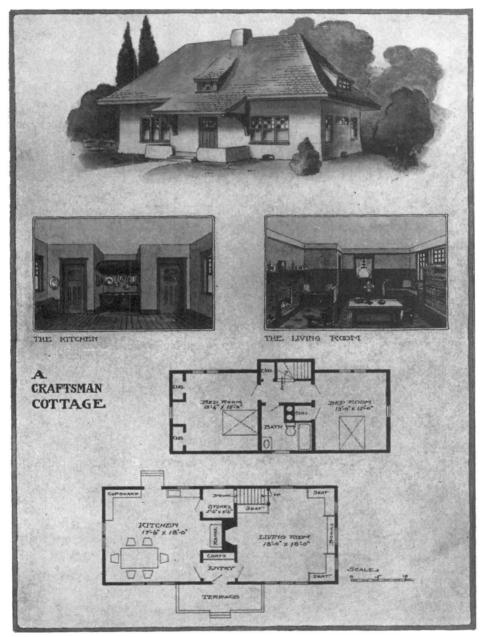

A CRAFTSMAN COTTAGE

Published in The Craftsman, April, 1905.

THE DRAWING OF THE EXTERIOR SHOWS THE GRACEFUL LINES AND PROPORTIONS OF THE COTTAGE. THE GLIMPSES GIVEN OF THE INTERIOR SHOW HOW A HOODED RANGE IS PLACED IN A RECESS AND THEREFORE OUT OF THE WAY IN THE ROOM WHICH SERVES AS KITCHEN AND DINING ROOM, AND ALSO HOW A LIVING ROOM MAY BE MADE INDIVIDUAL AND CHARMING AT VERY LITTLE COST.

SUBURBAN HOUSE DESIGNED FOR A LOT HAVING WIDE FRONTAGE BUT LITTLE DEPTH

Published in The Craftsman, September, 1905.

HOW THE HOUSE LOOKS WITH AMPLE GROUNDS AROUND IT AND A SETTING OF TREES FOR A BACKGROUND.

THIS house was designed primarily for use in the suburbs and the plan was adapted to a lot with wide frontage, but no great amount of depth. Of course, it would be better to have such a building surrounded by plenty of lawn, trees and shrubs; but if ground space were limited, a great deal could be made even of a meager allowance for front and back yards.

While the design admits the use of other materials which may be better suited to a given locality or considered more desirable by the owner, our plan was to have the house built of stone and shingles, the lower story and chimneys being of split field stone laid up in dark cement, and the upper story of cedar or rived cypress shingles, so finished that they are given a soft gray tone in harmony with the prevailing color of the stones. We have suggested that the shingle roof be stained or painted a soft moss green.

We regard the arrangement of these verandas as being especially comfortable and convenient, for although none of them are large, they serve admirably to supplement the inner rooms by furnishing what are practically outdoor rooms for general use. The front veranda, which is partially recessed, is sheltered from the street by the parapets and flower boxes. As doors open from this veranda into the hall, dining room and living room, it is much more closely connected with the house proper than is the case with the usual entrance porch, and is well fitted to serve as an outdoor sitting room. The veranda at the back of the house opens from the dining room and is meant to be used as a dining porch in summer time. Another door opening into the pantry makes it easy to serve meals out there. In winter this porch can easily be glassed in and used as a conservatory or sun room, and if heated, would make a very pleasant place for the serving of afternoon tea or for any such use. A third veranda opens from the kitchen and is meant especially for the comfort and convenience of the servants.

We would suggest here also that the openings from the hall into the dining room and living room be very much wider—a thing which could be easily done and which is now a feature of all the Craftsman houses. A glance at the floor plan will suggest the charm of such an arrangement, as it would allow a long vista from one fireplace to the other and would add much to the comfort and charm of the house as a whole. As will be noted, the liv-

20

SUBURBAN HOUSE FOR WIDE LOT WITH LITTLE DEPTH

ing room fireplace is flanked on either side by a built-in bookcase with a casement window above, and in the dining room the same arrangement furnishes two china closets surmounted by casements set high in the

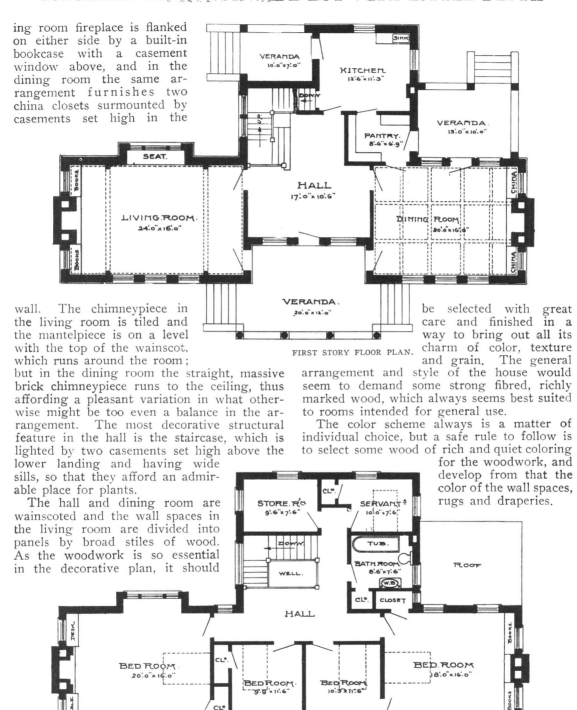

FIRST STORY FLOOR PLAN.

wall. The chimneypiece in the living room is tiled and the mantelpiece is on a level with the top of the wainscot, which runs around the room; but in the dining room the straight, massive brick chimneypiece runs to the ceiling, thus affording a pleasant variation in what otherwise might be too even a balance in the arrangement. The most decorative structural feature in the hall is the staircase, which is lighted by two casements set high above the lower landing and having wide sills, so that they afford an admirable place for plants.

The hall and dining room are wainscoted and the wall spaces in the living room are divided into panels by broad stiles of wood. As the woodwork is so essential in the decorative plan, it should be selected with great care and finished in a way to bring out all its charm of color, texture and grain. The general arrangement and style of the house would seem to demand some strong fibred, richly marked wood, which always seems best suited to rooms intended for general use.

The color scheme always is a matter of individual choice, but a safe rule to follow is to select some wood of rich and quiet coloring for the woodwork, and develop from that the color of the wall spaces, rugs and draperies.

SECOND STORY FLOOR PLAN.

21

SUBURBAN HOUSE FOR WIDE LOT WITH LITTLE DEPTH

PARTIALLY RECESSED ENTRANCE PORCH, SO SHIELDED BY PARAPETS AND FLOWER BOXES THAT IT MAY BE USED AS AN OUTDOOR LIVING ROOM.

CORNER OF THE LIVING ROOM, SHOWING STRUCTURAL EFFECT OF FIREPLACE AND THE BUILT-IN BOOKCASES SET FLUSH ON EITHER SIDE SO THAT THE TOPS ARE PRACTICALLY AN EXTENSION OF THE MANTEL.

A VERY SIMPLE AND INEXPENSIVE COTTAGE BUILT OF BATTENED BOARDS

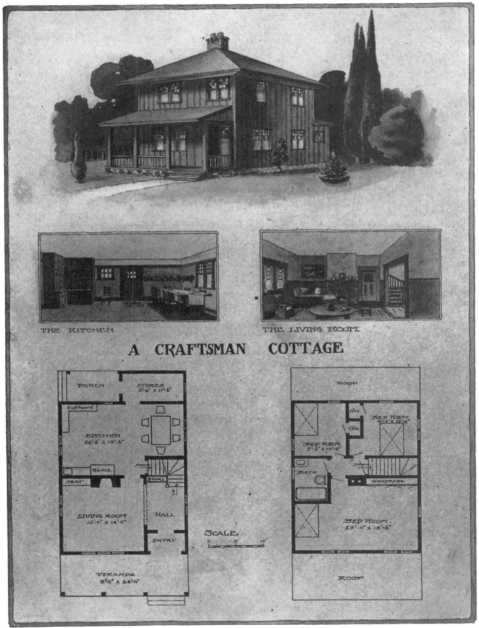

A CRAFTSMAN COTTAGE

Published in The Craftsman, April, 1905.

AN ILLUSTRATION OF THE DECORATIVE POSSIBILITIES OF SIMPLE BATTENED BOARDS. THE INTERIOR VIEWS CONTAIN ANOTHER SUGGESTION FOR THE ARRANGEMENT OF A COMBINED KITCHEN AND DINING ROOM AND ALSO SHOW HOW A VERY PLAIN LIVING ROOM MAY BE MADE COMFORTABLE AND HOMELIKE.

A CEMENT HOUSE THAT SHOWS THE DECORA-
TIVE USE OF CONCRETE AS A FRAMEWORK

Published in The Craftsman, January, 1907.

EXTERIOR VIEW.   NOTE EFFECT OF RAISED FRAMEWORK OF CONCRETE AGAINST ROUGH-CAST PANELS.

ONE or the other of the more massive forms of construction seems to be called for by the design of this house, which was meant to be built either of concrete or of hollow cement blocks, and so is planned especially with a view to the use of one or the other of these materials, although the design would be equally well suited to stone or brick. Believing that a house built of cement or concrete should be exceedingly simple in design, with plain straight lines and unbroken wall surfaces, we have carried out this idea as consistently as possible.

No timbers are used on the outside of the house, but the form of the framework is

A CEMENT HOUSE FRAMED IN SMOOTH CONCRETE

revealed in the heavy corner-posts, uprights and horizontal bands of smooth concrete which span the walls and break up the broad plain surfaces. As the walls are given a rough pebble-dash finish, this framework of smooth concrete, which projects slightly from the surface of the wall proper, gives a contrasting effect which adds much to the interest of the design. The concrete may either be left in the natural gray, or the coldness of this tint may be modified by an admixture of coloring which will give it a tone of deeper gray, a suggestion of green, or one of the buff or biscuit shades, according to the color effect that harmonizes best with the surroundings. If the house should be built of stone or brick, the color effect, of course, would be much more decided.

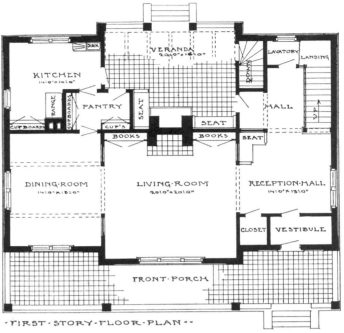

·FIRST·STORY·FLOOR·PLAN··

The roof is of slate—not the smooth, thin, lozenge-shaped slates with which we are so familiar, but a much more interesting form of this durable roofing material. The slates we have in mind are large and as rough on surface and edge as split paving-stones. They come in very interesting colors, dull red and slate-color with green and purplish tones which are much like the varied colorings found in stone. If red slate should be chosen for the roof, a pleasant repetition of the color could be obtained by flooring the verandas with square cement blocks of a dull brick red, which give the same effect as the much more expensive Welsh tiles.

Ample provision is made in this house for the healthful outdoor living that is now regarded as so necessary. A wide veranda extends across the entire front and at the back is a large square recessed porch that looks out over the garden at the rear of the house and is used as an outdoor living room where meals can be served if desired. This porch is exposed to the weather on one side only and this can easily be glassed in for the severest days of winter. With a southern exposure, though, it might be open nearly all winter, except on inclement days, for a sun room is pleasant when a room completely walled in is chilly and gloomy and in this case the

warmth of the sun would be supplemented by the comfort of the open fire, for the veranda is provided with an outdoor fireplace big enough to hold a pile of good sized logs. As this veranda has so much the character of a living room, the walls are treated in a way that connects it closely with the interior of the house. A high wainscot of cypress runs around all three sides and built-in fireside seats of the same wood afford a comfortable place for those who are minded to enjoy the fresh air and the warmth of the blazing logs at the same time. A fairly large table placed out here would serve all requirements for both living room and dining room out of doors, and a few comfortable easy chairs would make it a most inviting lounging place. The red cement floor would best be covered by a thick Indian blanket or two, or any rug of sturdy weave and primitive color and design. The wooden ceiling of the porch is heavily beamed and from the beams hang lanterns enough to make the place cheerful by night as well as by day. The color of the floor is repeated in the massive fireplace of hard-burned red brick and the plain mantel-shelf is made of a thick cypress plank.

Just above the sun room is an open-air sleeping room of the same size and general

25

A CEMENT HOUSE FRAMED IN SMOOTH CONCRETE

LIVING ROOM, SHOWING FIREPLACE AND BUILT-IN BOOKCASES WITH PANELS ABOVE. THE USE OF SPINDLES APPEARS IN THE GRILLES AND BALUSTRADE AND THE IDEA IS FURTHER DEVELOPED IN THE FURNITURE.

arrangement, except that it has no fireplace. On this upper porch the balustrade is replaced by a solid parapet made of the wall of the house. Like the sun room, this sleeping porch can be glassed in when necessary for protection from driving storms. But under ordinary circumstances no protection from the weather is needed even in winter, as nothing is better for the average housed-up human being than sleeping out of doors under plenty of covers.

The plan of the interior is an excellent example of the Craftsman method of arranging the divisions so as to secure at once the greatest possible amount of space, freedom and convenience within a given area and also to keep the construction as inexpensive as possible. The only fireplace is in the living room and is so placed that it may use the same chimney as the veranda fireplace. The ar-

rangement of the rooms, however, is so open that both dining room and reception hall share the benefit of the fireplace. Draughts from the entrance are cut off by a small vestibule which opens into the reception hall and the space beside it is occupied by a coat closet which receives wraps, overshoes and all those articles which are such a problem to dispose of in a hall that is part of the living room.

Ceiling beams are used only to indicate the divisions into rooms, but around the ceiling angle runs a broad beam and all three rooms are wainscoted to the height of six feet with oak paneling. We have suggested oak for the interior woodwork in this house, as the effect of it is both rich and restful and the color mellows with every passing year. Our idea would be to finish it in a rich nut-brown tone, which has much to do with giving a mellow sunny effect to the whole decorative

A CEMENT HOUSE FRAMED IN SMOOTH CONCRETE

scheme, for color goes far toward creating the cheery atmosphere that rightly belongs to a home. The rough plaster of the shallow wall spaces above the wainscot might be done in a warm tawny yellow and the whole decorative scheme developed from this foundation of walls and woodwork.

The structural feature that is most prominent in the living room is the fireplace, with the bookcase built in on either side. These bookcases are about four feet in height, so that the upper panels of the wainscot show above them. One decorative structural feature that is seen in all these rooms is the use of spindles wherever they would be effective. They appear in the balustrade of the staircase, in the open spaces above the panels, in the little partitions, in the continuation of these into grilles

above the doors, in the built-in seats and even in the furniure.

On the second story there are three large bedrooms in the front of the house and the open-air bedroom at the back. The staircase with its well occupies the space at one side of the sleeping porch, and the bath room is at the other. The upper hall, though not large, is so designed as to give a feeling of open arrangement and free communication, and the closets are concentrated at the center, where they are easy of access and do not interfere with the space required for the sleeping rooms. The plan of this house, as well as its decoration and interior arrangement, admit of very free interpretation and may be modified greatly to meet personal tastes and requirements.

VERANDA THAT IS FITTED UP AS A LIVING ROOM, SHOWING OUTDOOR FIREPLACE, WAINSCOTING, BUILT-IN SEATS AND USE OF LANTERNS, WITH SUGGESTIONS FOR SUITABLE FURNISHINGS.

CEMENT HOUSE SHOWING LAVISH USE OF HALF-TIMBER AS A DECORATION

Published in The Craftsman, January, 1909.

CRAFTSMAN HOUSE AT NASSAU, LONG ISLAND. NOTE THE EFFECT OF SLOPING FOUNDATION AND PARAPETS.

THE house illustrated on this page was not only designed in The Craftsman Workshops, but built largely under our own supervision, so that Craftsman ideas as to plan and construction have been carried out with only such modifications as were suggested by the individual tastes and needs of the owner. It is definitely a suburban residence and its site is as desirable as it well could be for the home of a man who wishes to have plenty of space and freedom in his surroundings and yet be within convenient reach of the city. The owner, a New York business man, is keenly desirous of making the part of Long Island which he has chosen for his home one of the most delightful places within the immediate neighborhood of New York: thus his interest has not been limited merely to the building of a desirable house, but has extended to the planning of its surroundings so that the place shall be beautiful as a whole.

The site is large enough to allow for extensive grounds, which are being laid out with direct reference to the plan of the house. There is a slope of about fifteen feet from the rear of the lot down to the front. This slope is terraced at the highest part and the house is built well to the rear, allowing for a large lawn and shrubbery in front. The terrace at the back is used for a vegetable garden and the rest of the lot is left so far as is possible in its natural shape.

The rising ground upon which the house is situated affords an extensive view over the hills and meadows of Long Island. The house faces directly southeast and at the west end is a terrace, covered with a pergola, which commands a view of the main road,—a busy thoroughfare that is usually thronged with carriages and automobiles. At the opposite end of the house is a porch which looks directly toward the neighboring golf links. This porch is connected with the dining room by double French doors so that in summer it can be used as an outdoor dining room, especially as it will be protected all around with screens. In winter the screens will be replaced with glass, so that the porch may be used as a sun room or as a breakfast room on mild days. The small front porch serves to shelter the entrance.

These porches and the pergola greatly relieve the severity of the plan. As the house is built of cement, the construction naturally calls for straight lines and massive effects; but while these are preserved in their entirety, all sense of coldness or bareness is avoided by the liberal use of half-timber and by such structural features as we have just described. The floors of the pergola, the entrance porch, the dining porch, and the small kitchen porch

28

CEMENT HOUSE WITH HALF-TIMBER DECORATION

at the rear of the house are all of dull red cement divided into squares so that they have more the appearance of Welsh quarries. All the exterior woodwork is cypress darkened to a warm tone of brown by the chemical process which is described fully in the chapter dealing with wood finishes.

Long shallow dormers on either side of the house serve to break the straight lines of the roof. The roof itself has widely overhanging eaves supported on heavy

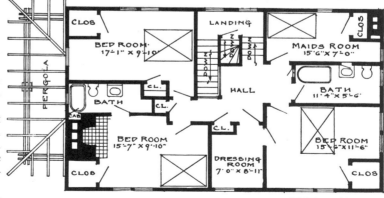

FIRST FLOOR PLAN

square timbers which project slightly and the whole upper story overhangs at the ends of the house, the weight being supported upon the projecting timbers. The line of demarcation between the upper and lower stories is emphasized by a wide timber which runs completely around the house. Above this are the smaller timbers which divide the cement wall into panels.

As the house is intended for a small family of three, with office accommodation for the owner, the interior arrangement is very simple. The entrance door leads directly into a central hall that opens into the dining room on one side and into the living room on the other, both openings being so wide that there is hardly any sense of division. The staircase is at the back of the hall, where a small coat closet is provided in a little nook taken off the space allowed for the butler's pantry.

Both living room and din-

ing room are closely connected with out of doors; the dining room, as we have already said, opening upon the screened porch and the living room upon the pergola. Just back of the living room is the den, which is the owner's special retreat and work-room. For this reason, double doors divide it from the living room instead of the usual broad opening. The big fireplace in the living room is so placed that the cheery glow of the fire is seen from both the hall and the dining room, as it forms one end of a vista which goes straight through to the dining porch. The built-in bookcase fills the space between this fireplace and the corner on one side, and on the other side is the door leading to the pergola. The entire front of the dining room is taken up with a built-in sideboard, flanked on either side by a china closet. Directly over this sideboard is the group of three windows which lights the dining room from the southeast.

The woodwork in the hall, living room and dining room is all of chestnut, fumed to a rich brown tone and given the soft dull finish that makes the surface appear fairly to radiate color. The fact that the woodwork is alike throughout these three rooms emphasizes the close connection between them and makes them appear almost like different parts of one room that is furnished harmoniously throughout.

SECOND FLOOR PLAN.

29

CEMENT HOUSE SHOWING CRAFTSMAN IDEA OF HALF-TIMBER CONSTRUCTION

Published in The Craftsman, August, 1906.

EXTERIOR VIEW SHOWING STRUCTURAL USE OF TIMBERS AND THE WAY WINDOWS ARE BANDED TOGETHER.

A house that typifies to rather an unusual degree the Craftsman idea of construction is shown here. It is a perfect square in plan and is designed with the utmost simplicity. There are no bays, recesses or projections on the outside, the attractiveness of the exterior depending entirely upon the proportions of mass and spacing. It is a building which should attain the maximum of durability for cement con-

CEMENT HOUSE SHOWING HALF-TIMBER CONSTRUCTION

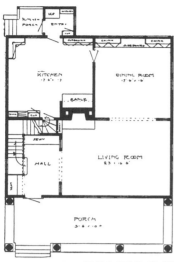

FIRST STORY FLOOR PLAN.

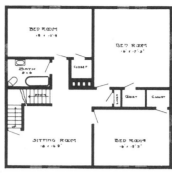

SECOND STORY FLOOR PLAN.

struction, as there is nothing to invite decay or render repairs necessary.

The walls are built of cement plaster and metal lath, the half-timber construction being used to break up the severely plain wall spaces into panels that are more agreeable to the eye. As originally designed the rough-finished cement was left in its natural gray color and the roof of white cedar shingles was merely oiled and left to weather to a harmonizing tone of silvery gray. The necessary color accent as well as the emphasis of form is given by the wood trim, which should be of cypress so treated that the brown color of the wood is fully brought out. The rafters of the porch as well as those supporting the widely overhanging roof are left uncased, carrying out the effect of solid construction which distinguishes the entire building and emphasizing the decorative use made of wood.

CORNER OF LIVING ROOM SHOWING FIREPLACE SET FLUSH WITH THE WALL AND HAVING PANEL OF DULL FINISHED PICTURE TILE. NOTE THE DECORATIVE EFFECT OF OPENINGS IN THE SPINDLE GRILLE WHICH APPEARS IN THE HALL, ALSO THE PLACING OF THE SEAT AND THE ARRANGEMENT OF THE STAIRCASE.

A COMFORTABLE AND CONVENIENT HOUSE FOR THE SUBURBS OR THE COUNTRY

Published in The Craftsman, May, 1907.

VIEW OF THE FRONT, GIVING A GOOD IDEA OF THE EFFECT OF BRICK AND CEMENT WALLS WITH TILED ROOF.

BELIEVING as we do that the happiest and healthiest life is that in the country, we take especial pleasure in designing houses that are definitely meant to be surrounded by large grounds that slope off into the fields, meadows and orchards all around. Such a house has always the effect of taking all the room it needs, and this will be found important when we come to analyze the elements that go toward making the restful charm of a home. The sense of privacy and freedom from intrusion that is conveyed by English homes with their ample gardens and buildings placed well back from the street is a quality which we badly need in our American home life as a relief from the rush and crowding outside.

Although the form of this house is straight and square, its rather low, broad proportions and the contrasting materials used in its construction take away all sense of severity. The walls of the lower story and the chimneys are of hard-burned red brick and the upper walls are of Portland cement plaster with half-timber construction. The foundation, steps

and porch parapets are of split stone laid up in dark cement and the roof is tiled. Of course, this is only a suggestion for materials, as the house would be equally well adapted to almost any form of construction, from stone to shingles. The coloring also may be made rich and warm or cool and subdued, as demanded by the surroundings. One feature that is especially in accordance with Craftsman ideas is the way in which the half-timbers on the upper story are used. While we like half-timber construction, it is an article of faith with us that it should be made entirely "probable"; that is, that the timbers should be so placed that they might easily belong to the real construction of the house. In a building that is entirely designed by ourselves we adhere very strictly to this rule, varying it only when the taste of the owner requires a more elaborate use of timbers, such as is shown in the house illustrated on page 28. Another feature of typical Craftsman construction is well illustrated in the windows used in this house. It will be noted that they are double-hung in places where they are ex-

A COMFORTABLE AND CONVENIENT SUBURBAN HOUSE

posed to the weather and that casements are used when it is possible to hood them or to place them where they will be sheltered by the roof of the porch.

The arrangement of the interior of this house is simplicity itself, as the living room and dining room, which have merely the suggestion of a dividing partition, occupy the whole of one side. The arrangement of kitchen, hall and staircase on the other side of the house is equally practical and convenient, as it utilizes every inch of space and provides many conveniences to lighten the work of the housekeeper.

The entrance door opens into a small vestibule that serves to shut off draughts from the hall, especially as the entrance from the vestibule to the hall is at right angles to the front door instead of being directly opposite, mak-

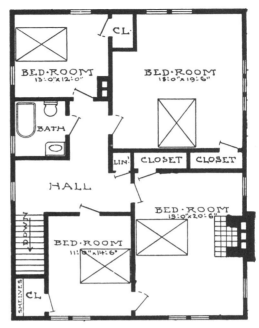

SECOND STORY FLOOR PLAN.

ing the danger from draughts so small that this opening might easily be curtained and a second door dispensed with. The broad landing of the staircase is opposite this opening from the vestibule and in the angle where the stair runs up a large hall seat is built. The vestibule jutting into the living room leaves a deep recess at the front, in which is built a long window seat just below the triple group of casements that appears at the front of the house. The fireplace is in the center of the room just opposite the hall, and another fireplace in the dining room adds to the comfort and cheer.

In a recess in the dining room somewhat similar to that at the front of the living room the sideboard is built in so that the front of it is flush with the wall and three casement windows are set just above it. The china cupboards built in on the opposite side are shown in two ways in the plan and illustration. In one the cupboard is built straight with the wall and in the other across the corner. Either way would be effective and the choice depends simply upon personal preference and convenience.

The tone of the woodwork would depend largely upon the position of the house and consequent exposure of the rooms. If they

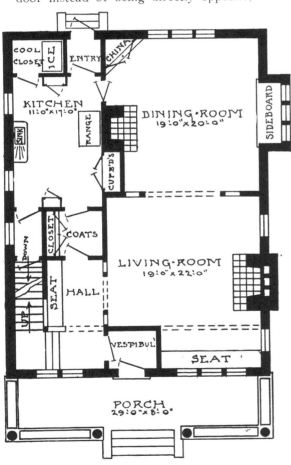

FIRST STORY FLOOR PLAN.

DETAIL OF ENTRANCE PORCH SHOWING HEAVY ROUND PILLARS, DECORATIVE USE OF REVEALED CONSTRUCTION IN THE ROOF, AND THE USE OF FLOWER BOXES.

are bright and sunny nothing could be better than the rich nut-brown of oak or chestnut with its strong sugggestion of green, as this gives a somewhat grave and subdued effect that yet wakes into life in a sunshiny room and shows the play of double tones of green and brown under a sheen that makes them seem almost luminous. If the rooms are fairly well shaded so that the effect of warmth would be desirable in the color, the woodwork might be of cypress, as its strong markings take on deep shades in the softer parts and beautiful autumn tints in the grain when treated by the Craftsman process that emphasizes so strongly the natural quality of the wood and brings out all its color.

A COMFORTABLE AND CONVENIENT SUBURBAN HOUSE

CORNER OF DINING ROOM SHOWING TILED CHIMNEYPIECE WITH COPPER HOOD; BUILT-IN CUPBOARD AND THE GROUPING OF WINDOWS AT THE SIDE.

LIVING ROOM WITH HALL BEYOND, SHOWING TYPICAL CRAFTSMAN DIVISION BETWEEN THE TWO ROOMS BY MEANS OF HEAVY SQUARE POSTS AND PANELS OPEN AT THE TOP.

A CRAFTSMAN CITY HOUSE DESIGNED TO ACCOM-MODATE TWO FAMILIES

Published in The Craftsman, October, 1907.
VIEW OF FRONT AND SIDE, INDICATING THE SIMILARITY IN ARRANGEMENT OF UPPER AND LOWER FLOORS.

SOME little time ago a problem was brought to us which proved interesting, not only in itself but on account of its application to a condition which in city life is almost universal. It was this: A man living in Brooklyn, who owned a lot thirty feet wide by a hundred feet deep, desired to build within this space a Craftsman house which should not only show a departure from the usual design of the city house in such matters as economy of space, arrangement of rooms, and interesting structural features that would serve as a basis for interior decorations and furnishing, but would accommodate two families who desired to live independently of one another, as they would in separate houses.

It had often been brought to our attention by people living in cities that most of our plans were for detached dwellings in the country or the suburbs, where the houses could have the environment of ample grounds and be given all the room necessary to carry out any idea of arrangement that might seem desirable. This method of living in the open with plenty of room and green growing things all around has always been so much more in accordance with the Craftsman idea of a home environment than any house cramped to fit the dimensions of a city lot, that our suggestions for house building have as a rule naturally taken the form of dwellings best fitted for the country. The number and frequency, however, of the requests which have come to us from time to time for city houses made the problem shown here one that we took much interest in working out.

As the owner desired a detached house with a walk on either side it was necessary to bring the dimensions of our plan within a very narrow space. Accordingly the width of the

A CRAFTSMAN CITY HOUSE DESIGNED FOR TWO FAMILIES

house was fixed at twenty-five feet, with a depth of sixty-eight feet, including a front porch nine feet in width. The first story is occupied by a tenant, the owner reserving the second floor for himself and his family.

It will be noticed by looking carefully at the floor plans that only the front porch, the vestibule and the rear entrance can be used in common by both families. There is no connection between the two apartments. One door from the vestibule opens to the stairway which leads to the second story and the other opens into the hall of the first story. Both stories are the same in arrangement and are planned to secure the greatest possible open-

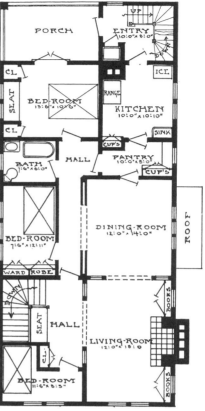

SECOND FLOOR PLAN.

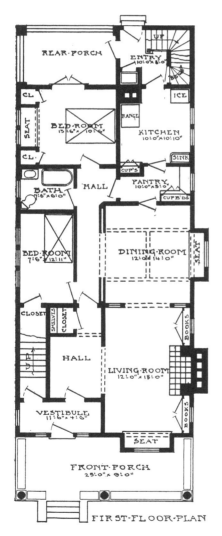

FIRST·FLOOR·PLAN

ness and freedom of space in the living rooms. The large bedrooms at the back of the house open upon rear porches, which are glassed in for the winter and screened in summer to serve as outdoor sleeping rooms.

The floor plans themselves give the best idea of the arrangement of space in the apartments. Both kitchens are provided with gas stoves and individual boilers for hot water. A dumbwaiter runs from the cellar to the attic for the convenience of the upper apartment. The cellar contains individual store rooms and coal bins, and a big laundry with a set of three tubs and a stove was installed, together with a hot water heating system for the entire house. The attic is divided in a way that provides two rooms in the dormer for the servants of both apartments, as well as a large room facing the front that can be used as a dry room in inclement weather or as a play-room for children. The cellar walls are of concrete faced with split field stone.

A CRAFTSMAN FARM HOUSE THAT IS COMFORT-ABLE, HOMELIKE AND BEAUTIFUL

Published in The Craftsman, June, 1906.

.VIEW FROM THE FRONT, SHOWING DORMER, GABLE AND RECESSED PORCH.   NOTE THE EFFECT OF THE BROAD LOW PROPORTIONS, THE GROUPING OF WINDOWS AND THE DECORATIVE USE OF TIMBERS.

A HOMELIKE AND BEAUTIFUL CRAFTSMAN FARMHOUSE

IF there is any one style of house that we enjoy planning more than others, it is a farmhouse,—a home that shall meet every practical requirement of life and work on the farm, and yet be beautiful, comfortable and homelike. This is our first farmhouse and we endeavored to make it characteristic in design, plan, decoration and the materials used for building. As a rule, we do not advocate the use of clapboards for sheathing the walls of a frame house, for the reason that the small, thin, smoothly planed and painted boards generally used for this purpose give a flimsy, unsubstantial effect to the structure and a characterless surface to the walls. However, clapboards are often preferred, especially in building a farmhouse, and it is quite possible to use them so that these objections may be removed. In this building the clapboards are unusually broad and thick, giving to the walls a sturdy appear-

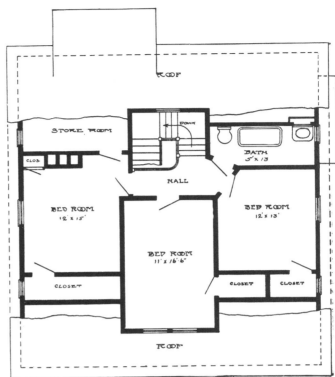

SECOND FLOOR PLAN.

FIRST FLOOR PLAN.

ance of permanence. They may be of pine, cedar, or cypress, and may be stained or painted according to individual taste and the character of the environment. If the house is to be rather dark and quiet in color, the boards might be given a thin stain of moss green or brown; or a delightful color effect may be obtained by going over the boards with a wash of much diluted sulphuric acid. With either one of these colors a good effect would be obtained by painting the timbers of the framework a light cream so that the structural features are strongly accented.

We regard this house as having in a marked degree the comfortable and inviting appearance which seems so essentially to belong to a home,—particularly to a farm home. It is wide and low, with rather a shallow pitch to the broad roof, the line of which is unbroken by the large dormers set at different

39

A HOMELIKE AND BEAUTIFUL CRAFTSMAN FARMHOUSE

CORNER OF LIVING ROOM, SHOWING TREATMENT OF WALL SPACES BY A VERY SIMPLE USE OF THE WOODWORK, WHICH IS USED TO GIVE THE EFFECT OF A BROAD, PLAIN FRIEZE. NOTE THE MANNER IN WHICH THE WINDOW AND DOOR FRAMINGS ARE RELATED TO THE LOWER BEAM OF THIS FRIEZE.

heights. The entrance porch, which is of ample size, is recessed to its full width. The timbers which accent the construction give special interest to the interior, as they are so placed as to add to the apparent width of the house, and are arranged so as to avoid, by means of the prominent horizontal lines of the beams, any possible "spotty" effect which might result if the vertical lines of the framework were not so relieved. This device is especially apparent in the grouping of the three windows which light the gable. The plan of the house makes it necessary that these be rather far apart, but they are built together by the beams so as to form a symmetrical group rather than to give the impression of three separate windows in a broad wall space. The same effect is preserved throughout the lower story by the massive beam which extends the entire width of the house, not only defining the height of the lower story but serving as a strong connecting line for the window and door framings which all spring from the foundation to the height of this beam.

A small vestibule, which serves to cut off draughts that might come from the entrance door, opens into the central hall which forms a connecting link between the living room on one side and the library and dining room on the other. The staircase, which is opposite the entrance, is placed well toward the back

CORNER OF DINING ROOM SHOWING SIDEBOARD BUILT INTO A RECESS, WITH GROUP OF WINDOWS AND DISH CUPBOARD.

of the house, giving as much width as possible to the hall. A small coat closet occupies a few feet of space that has been made available between the vestibule and the living room, so that the lines of both hall and living room are uninterrupted.

The living room has the advantage of every ray of sunshine which strikes that side of the house, as it is not sheltered by the porch. It is quite a long room in proportion to its width and the entire end at the rear is taken up by the fireplace and the two seats which, extending from it at right angles, give the effect of a deeply recessed fireside nook. A single chimney is made to do service for the entire house, as it is arranged to accommodate three flues.

HOUSE WITH COURT, PERGOLAS, OUTDOOR LIVING ROOMS AND SLEEPING BALCONIES

Published in The Craftsman, January, 1909.

HOUSE DESIGNED FOR OUTDOOR LIFE IN A WARM CLIMATE.

LIFE in a warm country, where there is much sunshine and where it is possible to be out of doors during the greater part of the time, was specially taken into consideration in the designing of this house, for the plan makes as much account of the terraces, porches and the open paved court as it does of the rooms within the walls of the building. Such a plan would serve admirably for a dwelling in California or in the Southern States, but would be advisable only for specially favored spots in the North and East, as its comfort and charm necessarily depend very largely upon the possibility of outdoor life.

As originally planned, the walls of the lower story are to be built of cement or of stucco on metal lath. The upper walls are shingled. The roof is of red tile and the foundation and parapets are of field stone. As with all these houses, though, the materials used are entirely optional and can be varied according to the taste of the owner, the requirements of the landscape or the limitations of the amount to be expended, as the building would look quite as well if constructed of concrete or of brick, and with clapboards in the place of shingles. If a

wooden house should be preferred, the walls from top to bottom could either be shingled or sheathed with wide clapboards, while the roof is equally well adapted to tiles, slates or shingles. The first of the perspective drawings gives a view of the whole house as seen from the rear, showing the pergola at the back and the design of the roof, which we consider specially attractive. The second drawing shows the side of the house instead of the front, as by taking this view it is possible to include both porch and court and also show the balcony and outdoor sleeping room on the upper story. A broad terrace runs across the front of the house and continues around the side, where it forms a porch which is meant to be used as an outdoor living room. This porch is nearly square in shape and is either tiled with Welsh quarries or, if a less expensive flooring be desired, is paved with red cement marked off into squares that measure about nine inches each way. This floor has a close resemblance to one made of Welsh quarries and is dry and durable. In flooring a porch of this kind it is always better to avoid the use of plain brick, as this porous material gathers and holds moisture to such an extent that the floor is seldom dry.

HOUSE WITH COURT, PERGOLAS AND OUTDOOR ROOMS

The entrance door opens from this porch into the hall, which is separated from the living room only by two panels open at the top after the usual Craftsman fashion, the wood running only a little above the height of the two bookcases, which may either be built in or movable, as desired. Directly opposite this entrance is the large fireplace, which is recessed so as to form a fireside nook. Seats are placed on either side and the tiled hearth extends the full length of these. Back of them, in the small recesses left on either side of the fireplace, are built-in bookcases with casement windows set above. A square bay window, below which is a broad window seat, looks out upon the terrace, and double glass doors from both living room and hall bring this part of the house into very close communication with the outside world; an important feature in the planning of a house intended for life in a warm climate where there is little rain.

The dining room has every appearance of being merely a large square recess in the living room, as the division between them is only indicated and the dining room is just large enough to afford comfortable accommodation for a good-sized dining table and the necessary furniture. The sideboard, which is built in, occupies the entire end of the room and a group of three casement windows are set in the wall just above it.

The floor plan shows the convenient arrangement of the hall, staircase and closets, everything being grouped within a small compass so that not an inch of space is wasted. The arrangement of pantry and kitchen is equally convenient and plenty of cupboard room is provided for dishes and the necessary kitchen utensils.

The chimney that is used for the kitchen range has space also for a flue leading from the fireplace on the porch outside. We are greatly in favor of these outdoor fireplaces, because there are many days and evenings when it is almost warm enough to stay out of doors, and yet without a fire it is not quite comfortable. Also, a fire in the open air has always something of the charm of a camp fire. The placing of this one is peculiarly

desirable, as it not only makes a pleasant sitting room of the porch, but also has much of the charm of a garden, as from the porch one steps down into the court, which is surrounded on the outside by a vine-covered pergola and which may be paved or not, as desired. Even when these courts are paved they often hold growing trees or a fountain, so that both shade and the nearness of green, growing things are possible, while the court itself seems merely an extension of the porch. The den, which can be closed off by doors from the rest of the house in case privacy is desired for work or reading, has double doors leading to the square entrance porch and also to the court.

On the second floor there are three large bedrooms, plenty of closet room and three baths. One of these is for the exclusive use of the maids and opens from the maids' room at the back. The other two are placed so

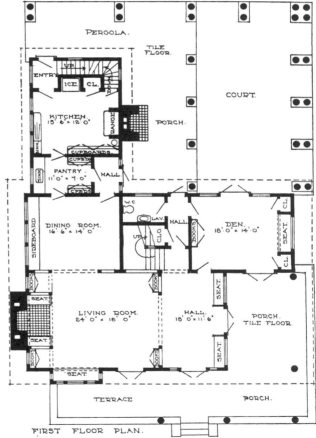

FIRST FLOOR PLAN.

HOUSE WITH COURT, PERGOLAS AND OUTDOOR ROOMS

CORNER OF HOUSE SHOWING PERGOLA AND SLEEPING PORCH.

that each one is accessible from two bedrooms, counting the outdoor sleeping room as one. The linen and clothes closets are so placed that they occupy the least possible amount of space. The central hall is more in the nature of a corridor running around the four sides of the staircase well, and at the back is a long window seat built beneath a group of windows that look out over the court and pergola.

The matter of interior woodwork and general scheme of color and decoration would depend very largely upon the part of the country in which the house is built. Its design is primarily that of a California house and reflects the spirit which rules the new architecture that is springing up in that country. Therefore it would seem quite in keeping to suggest that the inside of the house be finished after the well-known California style, because no other would be so completely in harmony with the plan of the exterior.

Living so much out of doors, the Californians almost instinctively make the transition between outdoors and indoors as little marked as possible by finishing the interior of their houses in the most natural way.

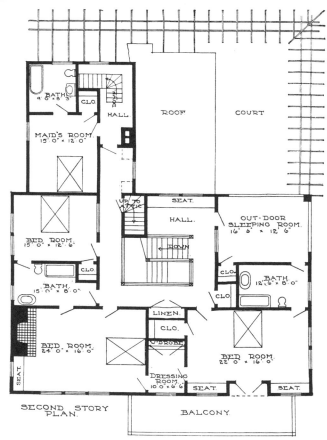

THE CRAFTSMAN'S HOUSE: A PRACTICAL APPLICATION OF OUR THEORIES OF HOME BUILDING

Fireplace in Open Air Dining Room

W HILE all the houses illustrated in this book are of Craftsman design, the dwelling shown here is perhaps the most complete example in existence of the Craftsman idea, for the reason that it is to be built by the founder and editor of The Craftsman at "Craftsman Farms," his estate in New Jersey, and will be used there as his own home. Therefore in this case the tastes of the designer are one with the tastes and needs of the owner, who has found no creative work more absorbingly delightful than this planning of a home which he intends to live in for the rest of his life. In addition to this it affords the opportunity for working out personally, in every practical detail, all the theories which have been applied to the houses of other people.

Craftsman Farms was apparently planned by nature for the site of just such a house. It has heavily wooded hills, little wandering brooks, low-lying meadows and plenty of garden and orchard land; and the house will be built on a natural terrace or plateau half way up the highest hill. The building faces toward the south, overlooking the partially cleared hillside, which runs down to the orchard and meadows at the foot and which needs very little cultivation to develop it into a beautiful sloping greensward with here and there a clump of trees or a mass of shrubbery. There is a friendliness about the natural conformation of the land which makes it seem homelike before one stone is laid upon another or one bit of underbrush is cleared away, for the combination of sheltering hills and woods with a sheltered swale or meadowland gives interesting

Entrance to Craftsman Farms

45

Published in The Craftsman, *October, 1908.*

FRONT VIEW OF THE HOUSE AT "CRAFTSMAN FARMS", SHOWING PERGOLA AND RECESSED ENTRANCE PORCH AND AT THE SIDE THE OUTDOOR DINING ROOM WITH FIREPLACE AND CHIMNEY BUILT AT THE END. THE PLASTER PANELS BETWEEN THE SEVERAL GROUPS OF WINDOWS ARE TO BE FILLED WITH LARGE PICTURE TILES SYMBOLIZING FARM LIFE AND INDUSTRIES.

variety in the immediate surroundings, while the view of the whole country from the hilltop through the gaps in the surrounding hills does away with any sense of being shut in.

In designing the house, the first essential naturally was that it should be suited exactly to the requirements of the life to be lived in it; the second, that it should harmonize with its environment; and the third, that it should be built, as far as possible, from the materials to be had right there on the ground and left as nearly as possible in the natural state. Therefore the foundation and lower walls of the building are of split field stone and boulders taken from the tumbledown stone fences and loose-lying rocks on the hillsides. The timbers are cut from chestnut trees growing on the land, and the lines, proportions and color of the building are designed with a special view to the contour of the ground upon

DETAIL OF LIVING ROOM SHOWING PIANO, PICTURE WINDOW AND BOOKCASES.

which it stands and the background of trees which rises behind it.

The hillside site, affording, as it does, well nigh perfect drainage, makes it possible to put into effect a favorite Craftsman theory,—that a house should be built without a cellar and should, as nearly as possible, rest directly on the ground with no visible foundation to separate it from the soil and turf in which it should almost appear to have taken root. The house is protected against dampness by making the excavation for the foundation down to clear hard soil, filling it in partly with the smaller pieces of stone that were rejected from the walls and placing on this a thick layer of broken stone leveled off with an equally thick layer of Portland cement and concrete, making it level and smooth like a pavement. All of this foundation is drain-tiled both inside and out. On the top of the cement floor is a double layer of damp-proofing, which extends without a break up the wall, and a thick layer of tar and sand, in which the floor timbers are bedded. Another layer of waterproof paper covers this; and then comes the floor itself—as completely protected from moisture as if it were on the top story of the building. The heating plant and laundry are provided for in a separate building and the stone storage

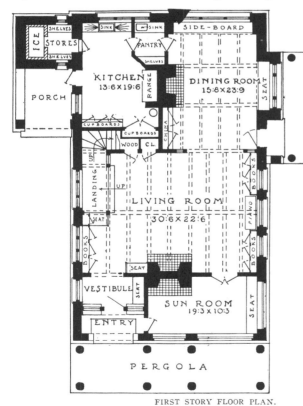

FIRST STORY FLOOR PLAN.

END OF LIVING ROOM, ILLUSTRATING HOW THE STAIRCASE WITH ITS LANDING MAY BE MADE THE PROMINENT STRUCTURAL FEATURE OF A ROOM.

vaults for vegetables and the like are sunk into the side of the hill.

No effort has been made to give the appearance of a grade line, the ground being allowed to preserve its natural contour around the stone walls of the first story. The upper walls are of plaster and half-timber construction. The plaster is given a rough pebble-dash finish and a tone of dull brownish green brushed off afterward so that the color effect varies with the irregularity of the surface. In each one of the large panels ultimately picture tiles will be set, symbolizing the different farm and village industries,—for example, one will show the blacksmith at his forge; another a woman spinning flax; others will depict the sower, the plowman and such typical figures of farm life. These tiles will be very dull and rough in finish and colored with dark reds, greens, blues, dull yellows and other colors which harmonize with the tints of wood and stone.

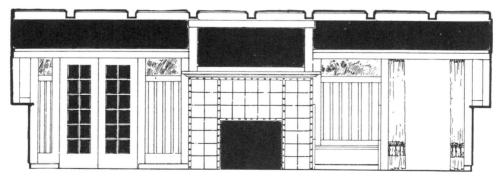

DETAIL OF LIVING ROOM SHOWING FIREPLACE, DOORS INTO SUN ROOM AND ENTRANCE TO VESTIBULE.

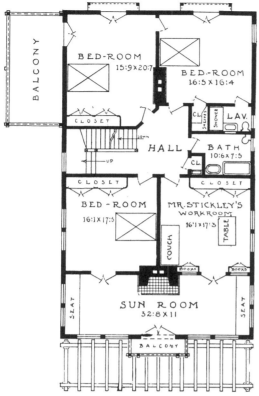

SECOND STORY FLOOR PLAN.

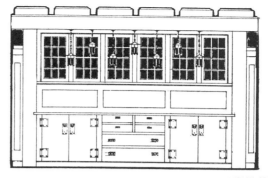

DETAIL OF DINING ROOM SHOWING
BUILT-IN SIDEBOARD AND WINDOWS.

proper, but is merely the expression of an individual fancy for an outdoor dining room and a sort of camp cooking place. At the end is built an outdoor fireplace and a big rough chimney. The detail of this fireplace, with its hobs, crane, and two brick ovens, is given in the first illustration.

The timbers are not applied to the outside of the house for the purpose of ornamentation, but are a part of the actual construction, which is thus frankly revealed. They are peeled chestnut logs squared on either side and with the face left rounded in the natural shape of the tree, hewn a little here and there to keep the lines from being exaggerated in their unevenness. These timbers are stained to a grayish brown tone that, from a little distance, gives the same effect as the bark. The lines of the red-tiled roof are low and broad, with an overhang of four feet on the ends and three feet at the sides.

The pergola is made of peeled cedar logs left in their natural shape and color, and the floor, which is almost on a level with the ground, is a dull red vitrified brick laid in herring-bone pattern at right angles. Extending from the side of the house is a roofed pergola,—if such a thing may be,—for while the timbers and the flooring are those of a pergola, it has a tiled roof like that of the house. This is not a part of the construction

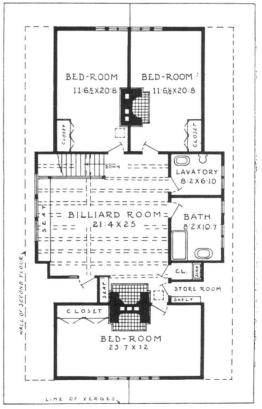

THIRD STORY FLOOR PLAN.

A SMALL SHINGLED HOUSE THAT SHOWS MANY INTERESTING STRUCTURAL FEATURES

Published in The Craftsman, February, 1907.

EXTERIOR VIEW FROM THE FRONT.

WE have suggested the use of shingles for the walls of this plain little cottage because they seem the best adapted to the peculiarities of its construction. They should, however, be laid in double course, the top ones being well exposed and the under ones showing not much over an inch below. This not only gives an interesting effect of irregularity as to the wall surface, but adds much to the warmth of the house. All the lines of the framework are simple to a degree, but the plainness is relieved by the widely overhanging eaves and rafters of the roof, the well-proportioned porch, which is balanced by the extension to the rear, the heavy beams which run entirely around the walls with a slight turn of the shingles above and the effective grouping of the windows. The little house is

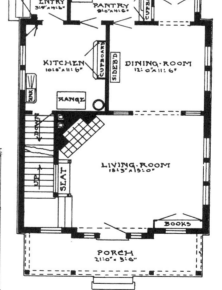

FIRST STORY FLOOR PLAN.

·WINDOW·SEAT·IN·LIVING·ROOM·

50

A SMALL SHINGLED HOUSE

·INTERIOR·ELEVATION·OF·LIVING·ROOM·
·FACING·FRONT·OF·HOUSE·

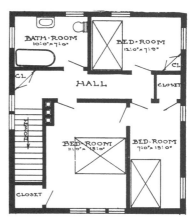

SECOND STORY FLOOR PLAN.

built to stand rough weather and this sturdiness is the direct cause of the wealth of attractive structural features. The roof of the porch projects two and a half feet, which affords protection even in a driving storm. Also for protection, all the exposed windows are capped by little shingled hoods which come up from the walls and which, in addition to their usefulness, form one of the most charming features of the whole construction. The eaves of the main roof project over the front for two and a half feet, and the weight is supported by purlins placed at the peak of the roof and at this connection with each of the side walls. This widely projecting roof gives a most comfortable effect of shelter and homelikeness, an effect which is heightened by the way

in which the quaint little casement windows on the second story seem to hide under its wing. The view of the living room shown in the illustration is that which would be seen by anyone looking through the triple casement on the side wall. The first thing seen by one entering from the porch would be the fireplace, which is thrown diagonally across the corner with a small built-in seat between it and the landing of the staircase. The fireplace is made of rough red brick, with a stone mantel-shelf set on a line with the wainscot.

LIVING ROOM SHOWING CORNER FIREPLACE, BUILT-IN SEAT AND STAIR LANDING, WITH A VIEW OF THE ENTRANCE DOOR AT THE SIDE.

A ROOMY, INVITING FARMHOUSE, DESIGNED FOR PLEASANT HOME LIFE IN THE COUNTRY

Published in The Craftsman, December, 1908.

VIEW SHOWING FRONT PORCH, OUTSIDE KITCHEN AND DORMER.

BELIEVING that no form of dwelling better repays the thought and care put upon it than does the farmhouse, we give here a design for the kind of house that is meant above all things to furnish a pleasant, convenient and comfortable environment for farm life and farm work.

The house is low, broad and comfortable looking in its proportions and exceedingly simple in design and construction. The walls are sheathed with clapboards and rest upon a foundation of field stone that is sunk so low as to be hardly perceptible, so that the house, while perfectly sanitary and well drained, seems very close to the ground. The clapboards are eight or ten inches wide and should be at least seven-eighths of an inch thick. Although they are to be laid like all clapboards, the thickness of the boards will necessitate a small triangular strip between each board and the joist to which it is nailed. This support prevents the boards from warping or splitting, as they might do if nailed directly to the joist without any support between.

The grouping of the windows is one of

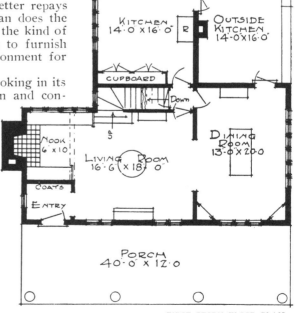

FIRST STORY FLOOR PLAN.

52

A ROOMY, INVITING FARMHOUSE

the most attractive features of the house as seen from the outside. They are all casements made to swing outward and are grouped in long horizontal lines that harmonize admirably with the low-pitched roof and the wide low look of the house as a whole. The shutters are made of wide clapboards like those used on the walls, four boards to each shutter, with a heart-shaped piercing cut out of the two central boards before they are fitted together. These shutters are wide enough to cover the whole window when closed. The windows that give light to the three front bedrooms upstairs are grouped into one long dormer, the casements being divided by two plaster panels, behind which come the ends of the partitions between the bedrooms. This dormer adds greatly to the effect of the whole building, as it breaks the long sweep of the roof without introducing a false line.

The plan of the interior is simple to a degree, as the rooms are arranged with a view to making the work of the household as light as possible. The greater part of the lower floor is taken up by the large living room, which practically includes the dining room, as the division between them is so slight as to be hardly more than the sug-

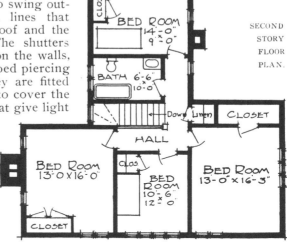

gestion of a partition on either side of the wide opening. The front door opens into an entry or vestibule which is divided from the living room by a curtain and, where provision is made, for hanging up hats and coats and for keeping other outdoor belongings.

LIVING ROOM OF THE FARMHOUSE SHOWING FIREPLACE NOOK WITH BUILT-IN SEATS AND CASEMENT WINDOWS; THE ENTRY APPEARS AT ONE SIDE OF THE NOOK.

A SIMPLE, STRAIGHTFORWARD DESIGN FROM WHICH MANY HOMES HAVE BEEN BUILT

Published in The Craftsman, January, 1909.

EXTERIOR VIEW, SHOWING WELL-BALANCED PROPORTIONS AND SIMPLE TREATMENT OF WINDOWS AND WALL-SPACES.

FIREPLACE IN LIVING ROOM, SHOWING THE BUILT-IN BOOKCASES AND CASEMENTS ON EITHER SIDE.

A SIMPLE, STRAIGHTFORWARD DESIGN

THIS has been one of the most popular of the Craftsman house designs and as shown here it has been modified somewhat from the first plan, the modifications and improvements having been suggested by the different people who have built the house, so that they are all valuable as the outcome of practical experience. Although the illustration shows plastered walls and a foundation of field stone, the design lends itself quite as readily to walls of brick or stone, or even to shingles or clapboards, if a wooden house be desired.

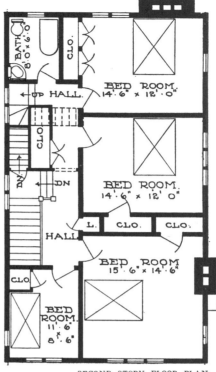

SECOND STORY FLOOR PLAN.

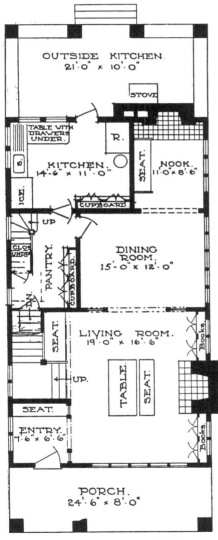

FIRST STORY FLOOR PLAN.

The outside kitchen at the back is recommended only in the event of the house being built in the country, because in town it would hardly be needed. In a farmhouse such an outside kitchen is most convenient as it affords an outdoor place for such work as washing and ironing, canning, preserving and other tasks which are much less wearisome if done in the open air. The position of the chimney at the back of the house makes it possible for a stove to be placed upon this porch for the use mentioned. The house is so designed that this outside kitchen may be added to it or omitted, as desired, without making any difference to the plan as a whole. The plan of the lower story shows the usual open arrangement of the Craftsman house. The entrance door opens into a small entry screened from the living room by heavy portiéres, so that no draught from the front door is felt inside. On the outside wall of the living room is the arrangement of fireplace and bookcases, as shown in the illustration. A large table might be placed in the center, with a settle back to it and facing the fire.

A CRAFTSMAN HOUSE IN WHICH TOWER CON-STRUCTION HAS BEEN EFFECTIVELY USED

Published in The Craftsman, September, 1906.

FRONT VIEW OF HOUSE SHOWING TOWERS AND VERANDAS IN FRONT AND PERGOLA AT THE SIDE.

SOMETHING of a departure is made from the usual style of the Craftsman house in planning this one, which we regard as one of the most completely successful house plans ever published in THE CRAFTSMAN. It is not a large house, yet it gives the impression of dignity and spa-ciousness which usually belongs only to a large building; it is in no sense an elaborate house, yet it is decorative,—possessing a sort of homely picturesqueness which takes away all appearance of severity from the straight lines and massive walls. This is largely due to the square tower-like construction at the

A CRAFTSMAN HOUSE WITH TOWER CONSTRUCTION USED

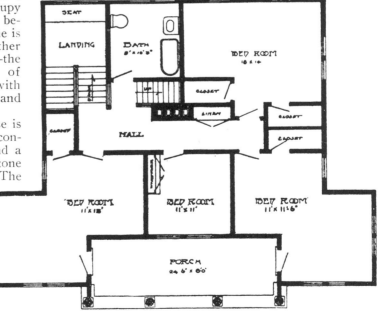

FIRST STORY FLOOR PLAN.

All the exterior wood trim is of cypress very much darkened by the chemical process which we use. In this house the exterior woodwork is especially satisfying in its structural form, being decorative in its lines and the division of wall spaces and yet obviously an essential part of the structure. The horizontal beams serve to bind together the lines of the whole framework, and the uprights are simply corner-posts and continuations of the window frames. The roof of dull red tiles gives life and warmth to the color scheme of the exterior, and the thick round pillars painted white lend a sharp accent that emphasizes the whole.

The entrance door is at the left end of the porch which, by this device, is made to seem less like a mere entrance and more like a pleasant gathering place where outdoor life may go on. This porch is illustrated in detail on page ninety-nine as a typical Craftsman front porch.

two corners in front and to the upper and lower verandas, both ample in size and deeply recessed, which occupy the whole width of the house between the towers. Of these, one is the entrance porch and the other an outdoor sleeping room,—the latter a very essential part of every house that is built with special reference to health and freedom of living.

As suggested here, the house is of cement and half-timber construction with a tiled roof and a foundation of local field stone carefully split and fitted. The foundation is carried up to form the parapets that shelter the recessed porches on the lower story, and the copings are of gray sandstone. The walls are of cement plaster on metal lath, the plaster being given the rough gravel finish and colored in varying tones of green.

SECOND FLOOR PLAN.   STORAGE-ROOM AND SERVANTS' ROOM IN ATTIC.

57

A CRAFTSMAN HOUSE WITH TOWER CONSTRUCTION

ALCOVE IN THE DINING ROOM MADE BY THE TOWER CONSTRUCTION. THIS LITTLE NOOK IS FITTED UP FOR A SMOKING ROOM OR DEN AND HAS ALL THE ADVANTAGES OF A BAY WINDOW OR SMALL SUN ROOM, AS THE WINDOWS ON EITHER SIDE ADMIT FLOODS OF SUNSHINE, PROVIDED THE HOUSE IS SO PLACED AS TO GIVE THIS TOWER A SOUTHERN OR WESTERN EXPOSURE. NOTE THE CONSTRUCTION OF THE OVERHEAD BEAMS.

A CRAFTSMAN HOUSE WITH TOWER CONSTRUCTION

A CORNER OF THE LIVING ROOM, LOOKING INTO THE DINING ROOM SO THAT THE POST-AND-PANEL CONSTRUCTION WHICH INDICATES A DIVISION BETWEEN THE TWO ROOMS IS PLAINLY SHOWN. THE CHIMNEYPIECE IS MADE OF LARGE SQUARE TILES, MATT-FINISHED IN A DULL TONE OF BROWNISH YELLOW AND BOUND AT THE CORNERS WITH STRIPS OF EITHER COPPER OR IRON. THE FIREPLACE HOOD IS OF COPPER AND THE ANDIRONS OF WROUGHT IRON. COMBINED WITH THE BROWN OF THE OAK OR CHESTNUT WOODWORK, THIS WOULD FORM THE BASIS OF A RICH AND QUIET COLOR SCHEME.

A CONCRETE COTTAGE DESIGNED IN THE FORM OF A GREEK CROSS TO ADMIT MORE LIGHT

Published in The Craftsman, February, 1907.

FRONT VIEW OF THE COTTAGE SHOWING THE TWO SMALL ENTRANCE PORCHES.

CONCRETE or hollow cement block construction were what we had in mind in the designing of this cottage. Therefore the form of it is especially adapted to the use of this material, although, like the others, the general plan admits of the use of brick or stone, clapboards or shingles, if desired. As we have shown it here, the side walls are broken into panels by raised bands of concrete, which bind the corners and also run around the entire structure at the connection of the roof and again between the first and second stories. These bands are smooth-surfaced, but the walls are made very rough by the simple process of washing off the surface with a brush and plenty of water immediately after the form is removed and while the material is set but still friable. If this is done at exactly the right time, the washing-brush can be so applied as to remove the mortar to a considerable depth between the blocks, leaving them in relief and producing a rough coarse texture that is very interesting.

The plan of this house is not unlike a Greek cross, the rooms being so arranged that the greatest possible allowance of space is made

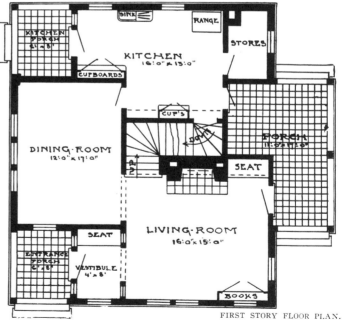

FIRST STORY FLOOR PLAN.

A CONCRETE COTTAGE

available and also an unusual amount of light and air. The foundation is of concrete and is continued upward on a gentle slant from the ground to a line at the base of the windows on the first floor, which gives a continuous horizontal line on a level with the parapets of the porches that are placed on either side of the front wing.

The main entrance porch is at the right of the house, as shown in the half-tone illustration, while the kitchen is entered from the porch on the left. The rear porch is recessed and extends the whole width of the wing, being large enough to serve as a very comfortable dining room. For this style of house we would recommend that all the porches be floored with red cement divided into squares. As shown in the illustration of the interior, the rooms on the first floor are separated with the open post-and-panel construction, which merely indicates a division between them.

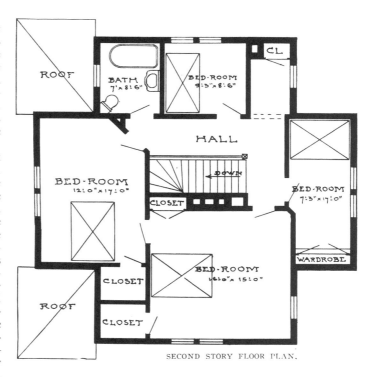

SECOND STORY FLOOR PLAN.

A SECTION OF THE LIVING ROOM, SHOWING ENTRANCE HALL, STAIRWAY, CHIMNEYPIECE, FIRESIDE SEAT AND A GLIMPSE OF THE DINING ROOM. NOTE THE WAY THE WOODWORK IS USED TO CARRY THE SAME STRUCTURAL IDEA THROUGHOUT THE WHOLE LOWER FLOOR.

A BUNGALOW OF IRREGULAR FORM AND UNUSU-
ALLY INTERESTING CONSTRUCTION

Published in The Craftsman, April, 1907

VIEW OF THE BUNGALOW SHOWING COURT AND PERGOLA, DINING PORCH AND SLOPE OF THE HILL.

THE plans and drawings of this bungalow, while partly our own, are adapted from rough sketches sent us by one of our subscribers, Mr. George D. Rand, of Auburndale, Mass. Mr. Rand is an architect who has retired from active work, and these sketches were made for his own bungalow, which is situated in the mountain region of New Hampshire. In sending us the sketches, Mr. Rand kindly gave us permission to use the idea as outlined by him, with such alterations as seemed best to us. In accordance with this permission, we make quite a number of minor modifications in the original design, and many of the suggestions for construction are our own.

The house is somewhat irregular in design, but is so admirably proportioned and planned that the broken lines impress one as they do when seen in some old English house that has grown into its present shape through centuries of alteration in response to changing needs. It seems above all things to be a house fitted to crown a hilltop in the open country, especially where the slope is something the same as indicated in the site here shown. The line from the back of the roof down to the boat landing comes as near to being a perfect relation of house and ground as is often seen, and this relation is of the first importance in the attempt to suit a house to its environment.

The exterior walls and the roof are of shingles, and the foundations, parapets, columns and chimneys are of split stone laid up in dark cement. The construction of the roof is admirable and, with all the irregularity, there is a certain ample graciousness and dignity in line and proportion. At the front of the house between the two gables is a recessed court, paved with red cement cut into squares like tiles and roofed over with a pergola of which the beautiful construction is shown in the detail given of this court.

The large porch at the side of the house is intended for an outdoor living and dining room and corresponds closely in arrangement with the rooms which open upon it. Its construction is the same as that of the court, except that it is sheltered by a wide-eaved roof instead of a pergola and is so arranged that it can be easily closed in for cold or stormy weather. At the end next the living room there is a large fireplace built of split stone, which exactly corresponds with the fireplace in the indoor living room. A good fire of logs on this outdoor hearth gives the same effect of warmth and cheer as a camp fire. If casements were placed all around the porch so that it could be entirely closed in time of storm and cold, it might be an excellent idea to floor it smoothly with wood for dancing; but if

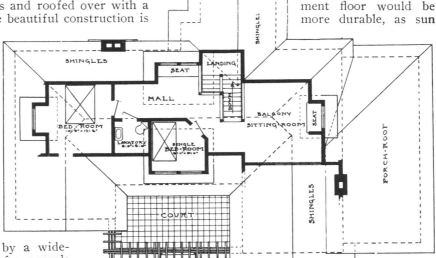

it is to be exposed to the weather, the cement floor would be more durable, as sun

·SECOND·FLOOR·AND·ROOF·PLAN·

and wind soon roughen the best wood floor.

The house is rich in fireplaces, for not only are there the large chimneypieces, in the living room and on the porch adjoining, but two of the bedrooms on the lower floor have corner fireplaces. As the kitchen is so placed as to be practically detached from the remainder of the house, another flue is necessary for the kitchen range.

From the court the entrance door opens into a small square hall, which is practically an alcove of the living room and which connects by a narrow passage with the bedrooms at the opposite side of the house. The bathroom is placed almost in the center of the house, which might be undesirable if it were not completely shut off from the living rooms by the plan of the hall and by the same plan made easily accessible to the three bedrooms.

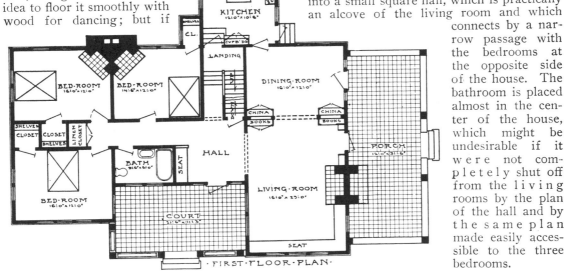

·FIRST·FLOOR·PLAN·

DETAIL OF THE COURT, SHOWING CONSTRUCTION OF THE PERGOLA AND THE USE OF VINES, SHRUBS AND FLOWER BOXES. THE GLASS DOOR IS THE MAIN ENTRANCE DOOR OF THE HOUSE.

The construction of the living room is very interesting, as everything is revealed up to the ridge pole and rafters of the roof. The roof itself has such a long sweep that there would be danger of its sagging, were it not for the trusses that brace it in the center. These trusses, in addition to their use, add much to the decorative effect of the structure. Across the front and down the side of the living room to the fireplace is a built-in seat paneled below and backed with a wainscot of V-jointed boards. If desired, the top of this seat can be hinged in sections, making the lower part a place for storing things. The window above the seat in front gives an unusually interesting effect, as there is a group of double casements on what in an ordinary house would be the lower floor, and another group of single casements, the center one higher than the sides, just above the frieze and beam. Another casement set high

in the wall is placed opposite the fireplace, corresponding in position to the door which opens upon the porch.

Extending to a point half way across the opening into the hall is the balcony which forms the upstairs sitting room; this is divided from the living room only by a railing. The floor of this balcony forms the ceiling of the dining room, which is separated from the living room only by double cupboards made to be used as bookcases on one side and china closets on the other. These cupboards extend to the same height as the window-sills and mantel, carrying this line around the room. The space above is open and hung with small curtains. This effect of a small low dining room recessed from a living room that runs clear to the roof is delightful in the sense it gives of homelike comfort, as the effect is that of a snug little retreat devoted to good cheer.

A BUNGALOW OF IRREGULAR FORM

CORNER OF THE LIVING ROOM, SHOWING UPPER AND LOWER WINDOWS AT THE FRONT OF THE HOUSE, THE SEAT WHICH SERVES BOTH AS WINDOW AND FIRESIDE SEAT AND THE FORM AND CONSTRUCTION OF THE FIREPLACE.

A PORTION OF THE LIVING ROOM, LOOKING INTO THE DINING ROOM. THE CEILING OF THE LATTER IS FORMED BY THE FLOOR OF THE BALCONY ABOVE, SO THAT IT HAS THE APPEARANCE OF A LOW-CEILED RECESS, AND THE BOOKCASES MAKE THE PARTITION. THE BALCONY IS USED AS AN UPSTAIRS SITTING ROOM.

A ROOMY, HOMELIKE FARMHOUSE FOR LOVERS OF PLAIN AND WHOLESOME COUNTRY LIFE

Published in The Craftsman, March, 1909.

BOTH in exterior seeming and in interior arrangement and finish, this building is essentially a farmhouse,—not of the comfortless type that we have been accustomed to of late years, but one that is reminiscent of earlier days, when a farmhouse was in very truth the homestead and as such was large, substantial, comfortable and inviting. The design is very simple, with clapboarded or shingled walls and a broad sheltering roof, the straight sweep of which is broken by a large dormer on either side. The wide veranda in front is recessed, forming a sheltered porch that could be used for much outdoor life. The windows as suggested here are all casements, those on the upper story being protected from the weather by the broadly overhanging roof and the lower ones sheltered by hoods. At the front of the house the dormer is extended to form a good-sized sleeping porch and at the back it accommodates the bathroom.

As the general effect of the house is broad and low, it is fitting that very little of the foundation should be visible. A far better effect is given if no attempt is made to establish too strict a grade line, as the house seems to fit the

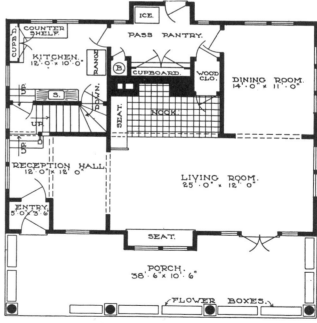

FIRST STORY PLAN

66

ground much better if the foundation is accommodated to the natural irregularities and if the floor of the porch is very little elevated above the turf.

The interior arrangement, while simplicity itself, is very convenient. There is hardly anything to mark the divisions between the reception hall, living room and dining room, so that these names rather serve to indicate the uses to which the different parts of this one large room may be put than to imply that they are separate rooms. In the very center of the house is the large fireplace nook which naturally forms the center of interest and attraction, with its ample chimneypiece of the split field stone and the comfortable fireside seat beside the hearth. Were it not for the arrangement of this large open space, there might be a sense of bareness; but this is entirely obviated by the shape of the room, the prominence given to the fireside nook, and the liberal use of wood in the form of beams, wainscots, seats and such built-in fixtures as may be necessary.

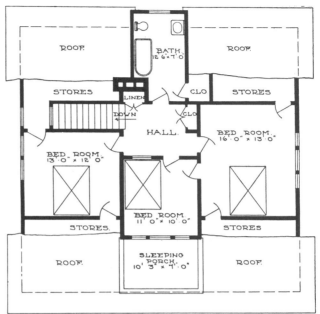

SECOND STORY PLAN.

FIRESIDE NOOK, GIVING AN IDEA OF THE BROAD CHIMNEYPIECE BUILT OF SPLIT FIELD STONE AND OF THE FIRESIDE SEAT, WHICH IS MADE OF WIDE BOARDS V-JOINTED.

67

A PLASTER HOUSE UPON WHICH WOOD HAS BEEN LIBERALLY USED

Published in The Craftsman, December, 1906.

FRONT OF THE HOUSE, SHOWING EFFECT OF PORCHES WITH WOODEN BALUSTRADES.

WE have always found the combination of rough-finished plaster with plenty of exterior woodwork to be very attractive, and this house is a good example of the way in which we relieve the severity of the plain plaster. The design of the house is not as straight and massive as is usual with the Craftsman cement or plaster houses, yet it is very simple, and the exterior features are such as to make for great durability.

The foundation of the house as shown is of very hard and rough red brick as to the visible part. Should this brick not be easily obtainable or too costly in the local market, a quarry-faced, broken-joint ashlar or some darker stone would be very effective with either gray or green cement. As to the woodwork, we would suggest cypress, which is inexpensive, durable and beautiful in color and grain when finished according to the process we describe elsewhere in this book. The color under this treatment is a rich warm brown which, when used for the half-timber construction, window framings and balustrades, would look equally well with plaster either left in the natural gray or given a tone of biscuit color or of dull green.

Some idea of the interior woodwork is given in the detail drawings. A great deal of wood is used in the form of wainscoting, grilles and

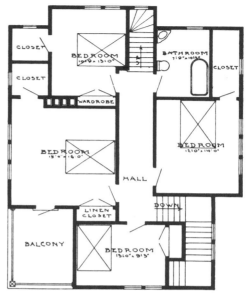

SECOND STORY FLOOR PLAN.

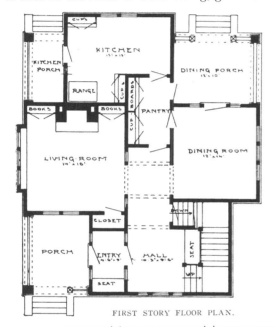

FIRST STORY FLOOR PLAN.

the like, and the whole scheme of decoration and furnishing naturally is founded on this use of wood. It would be best to treat the upper walls and ceilings of the hall, living room and dining room alike, as the object is to give a sense of space, dignity and restfulness to the part of the house that is most lived in and this effect is best obtained by having no change in the background. The rooms open into each other in such a way as to suggest one large room irregularly shaped and full of recesses, and any marked difference in the treatment of the walls is apt to produce an effect of patchiness as well as the restlessness that comes from marked variations in our home surroundings.

DETAIL DRAWING SHOWING CONSTRUCTION AND PLACING OF WAINSCOT, DOOR, STAIRCASE AND LANDING.

A FARMHOUSE DESIGNED WITH A LONG, UN-BROKEN ROOF LINE AT THE BACK

Published in The Craftsman, January, 1909.

FRONT VIEW, SHOWING RUSTIC PERGOLA AND INTERESTING CONSTRUCTION THAT SUPPORTS THE OVERHANG.

REAR VIEW SHOWING WIDE SWEEP OF ROOF AT THE BACK IN PLACE OF THE CUSTOMARY "LEAN-TO."

A FARMHOUSE WITH A LONG ROOF LINE

WE feel that the design for this farmhouse is one of the most satisfactory that we have ever done, not only because the building, simple as it is, is graceful in line and proportion, but because the interior is so arranged as to simplify the work of the household and to give a good deal of room within a comparatively small area.

The plan is definitely that of a farmhouse, and in this frank expression of its character and use lies the chief charm of the dwelling. The walls might be covered with either shingles or clapboards, according to the taste and means of the owner. If the beauty of the building were more to be considered than the expense of construction, we should recommend the use of rived cypress shingles, as these are not only very durable but have a most interesting surface. The only difficulty is that they cost about double the price of the ordinary shingles. As the construction of the house in front is such that a veranda

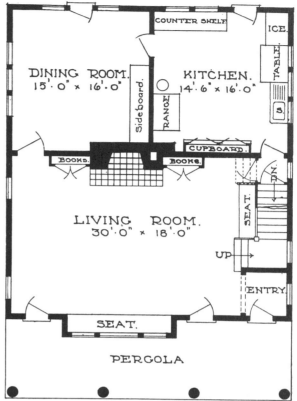

FIRST STORY FLOOR PLAN.

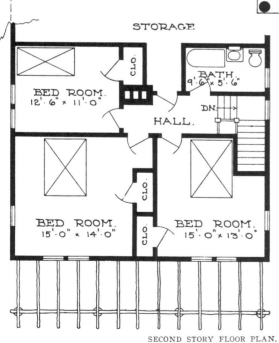

SECOND STORY FLOOR PLAN.

would be rather a disfigurement than an improvement, we have supplied its place by a terrace covered with a pergola. The terrace would naturally be of cement or vitrified brick and the construction of the pergola should be rustic in character. One great advantage of such a pergola is that the vines that cover it afford sufficient shade in summer, while in winter there is nothing to interfere with the air and sunlight, which should be admitted as freely as possible to the house. We have allowed the roof to come down in an unbroken sweep toward the back because of the beauty and unusualness of this long roof line as compared with the usual square form of a house with the lower roof of a porch or lean-to at the back. Furthermore, by this device there is considerable space for storage left over the kitchen and dining room. The entry opens into the living room at right angles with the entrance door and this opening might be curtained to avoid draughts.

TWO INEXPENSIVE BUT CHARMING COTTAGES FOR WOMEN WHO WANT THEIR OWN HOMES

IT has always seemed to us that if there is one kind of dwelling that is more generally needed than another, it is the small and inexpensive, yet comfortable and homelike, cottage that can be built almost for the year's rent of a flat, or even of room and board in a boarding house, and that would serve as a home for two or three people. Especially is this sort of a house needed by women of limited means,—women who either work at home or possibly in an office or shop and who need all the home comfort they can get, instead of dragging out an existence in a boarding house or facing the bugbear of rent day in a flat.

These cottages each would serve to accommodate a group of three or four and the number might even be stretched to six in case of very congenial people who did not mind

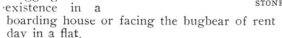

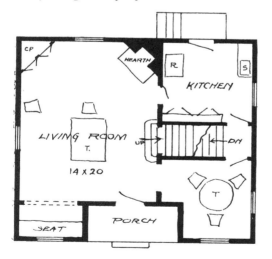

Published in The Craftsman, March, 1904.

STONE COTTAGE WITH RECESSED PORCH.

sharing their rooms. The houses as represented here are built of field stone, but the designs would serve equally well for concrete, —a form of construction that would greatly lessen the cost,—or for frame houses covered with shingles, clapboards, or even with plain boards and battens. In fact, after the initial cost of the lot in some suburb not too far away from the place of employment, it should be a very easy matter for two or three women who felt that they would like to make a home for themselves to combine their resources and build one of these little houses. Even the cost of the lot might be very greatly lessened if it were possible to build in a village near the city or right out in the country. It is the woman who is stranded in some forlorn hall bedroom, or who is forced to feel that she is a superfluous member of someone else's family, who would most welcome the dignity and content that would be found

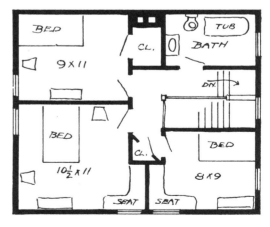

FIRST STORY FLOOR PLAN.

SECOND STORY FLOOR PLAN.

TWO INEXPENSIVE BUT CHARMING COTTAGES

in a home of her own,—a home which might be shared by a relative or close friend in similar circumstances.

The chief value of these little houses lies in the fact that although they are but the simplest of cottages, they nevertheless possess a beauty and individuality which is lacking in many a residence that costs ten times as much. We feel that in exterior attractions they are fitted to take rank with any of the houses designed in The Craftsman Workshops, and that the interior arrangement is compact and comfortable to a degree. The chief difference between them, as regards the exterior, lies in the fact that in the case of the first one the porch is recessed and, in the second, is extended to the dimensions of a good-sized veranda that runs the whole width of the house. In interior arrangement they are much alike, the living room in each case occupying the whole of one side of the house and

Published in The Craftsman, March, 1904.

STONE COTTAGE WITH VERANDA. NOTE THE EFFECT OF SQUARE BUN-GALOW ROOF AND OF CASEMENT WINDOWS HIGH UNDER THE EAVES.

opening into a dining alcove which takes about half of the other side. The kitchen occupies the remaining corner and, if this be fitted with convenient cupboards, work table and the like, there would be no necessity for a pantry. Upstairs also the arrangement of the two cottages is somewhat similar, as in each case the space is divided into three bedrooms and a bathroom, with plenty of closet room tucked away into nooks and corners.

As to the interior woodwork and furnishing, these need not be costly in order to be attractive. Some inexpensive native wood, such as pine, or cypress, or that grade of chestnut known to builders as "sound wormy," would, if finished properly, give the most delightful effect when used for interior trim, built-in seats, cupboards, balustrades for the stairways, and for wainscoting, —providing the sum set aside for the house admitted such a luxury as the last. The remaining wall spaces and the ceilings could be left in the rough sand-finished plaster, tinted in any color desired, and the fireplace would naturally be of brick or field stone and of the simplest design. Given such a foundation, the question of furnishing would adjust itself.

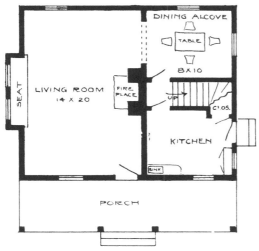

FIRST STORY FLOOR PLAN.

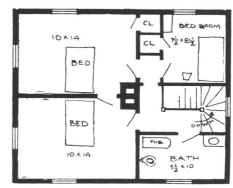

SECOND STORY FLOOR PLAN.

A LOG HOUSE THAT WILL SERVE EITHER AS A SUMMER CAMP OR A COUNTRY HOME

Published in The Craftsman, March, 1907.

EXTERIOR OF LOG HOUSE, SHOWING DECORATIVE USE OF THE PROJECTING ENDS OF PARTITION LOGS.

SO many people like log houses for summer homes that we give here a design that would harmonize with the most primitive surroundings. At the same time it is so carefully planned and so well constructed that it could be used as a regular dwelling all the year round. While the lines of the building are simple to a degree, all the proportions are so calculated and the details of the construction so carefully observed that, with all this simplicity and freedom from pretense, there is no suggestion of bareness or crudity. It is essentially a log house for woodland life, and it looks just that; yet it is a warm, comfortable, roomy building perfectly drained and ventilated and, with proper construction, ought to last for many generations.

As the first step towards securing good drainage and also saving the lower logs of the wall from decay, there is an excellent foundation built of stone or cement,—according to the material most easily and economically obtained,—and this foundation is quite as high as it would be in any dwelling built of the conventional materials in the conventional way. But as the appearance of such a foundation would spoil the whole effect of the house by separating it from the ground on which it stands, it is almost entirely concealed by terracing the soil up to the top of it and therefore to the level of the porch floors. The first log of the walls rest directly upon this foundation and is just far enough above the ground to prevent rotting. By this device perfect healthfulness is secured so far as good drainage is concerned, and at the same time the wide low house of logs appears to rest upon the ground in the most primitive way.

The logs used in building should have the bark stripped off and then be stained to a dull grayish brown that approaches as closely as possible to the color of the bark that has been removed. This does away entirely with the danger of rotting, which is unavoidable when the bark is left on, and the stain removes the raw, glaring whiteness of the peeled logs and restores them to a color that harmonizes with their surroundings. The best logs for this purpose are from trees of the second growth, which are easily obtained almost anywhere. They should be from nine to twelve inches in diameter and should be carefully

74

selected for their straightness and symmetry.

The wide porches that extend all along both sides of the house afford plenty of room for outdoor living. As shown in the picture, one end of the porch at the front of the house is recessed to form a square dining porch, which opens into the kitchen and also into the big room. This is a combined living room and indoor dining room, to be used for the latter purpose only in chilly or stormy weather, if the house is meant for a summer camp.

The general effect of this room is in exact harmony with the exterior of the house. The door from the porch opens into an entry which on one side gives access to the two bedrooms at the front of the house and on the other leads by a wide opening into the main room. The walls and partitions are of logs and the ceiling is beamed with logs flattened on the upper side to support the floor above. The fireplace, like the chimney outside, is built of split stone, a material especially suited to this house, and is in a nook or recess that is formed, not by the shape

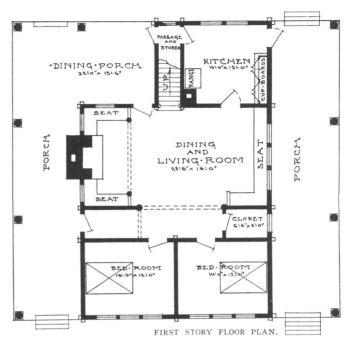

FIRST STORY FLOOR PLAN.

of the room, but by the suggestion of a division made by the two logs placed one above the other across the ceiling logs, and the two posts that form the ends of the fireside seats.

VIEW OF LIVING ROOM, SHOWING THE LOG CONSTRUCTION WHICH SEPARATES THE FIREPLACE NOOK FROM THE REST OF THE ROOM, AND ALSO GIVING AN IDEA OF THE EFFECT TO BE OBTAINED BY THE USE OF LOG PARTITIONS.

A PLEASANT AND HOMELIKE COTTAGE DESIGNED FOR A SMALL FAMILY

Published in The Craftsman, February, 1905.

VIEW OF COTTAGE FROM THE FRONT.

FIREPLACE AND SEAT IN THE LIVING ROOM, WITH GLIMPSE OF HALL AND STAIRCASE.

COTTAGE FOR A SMALL FAMILY

THIS design for a cottage is best suited for the suburbs or for a village, as the shape of the building is such that it needs plenty of ground around it. If it were built in the open country, it would look particularly well on a large lot where there are plenty of trees, as for example the site of an old apple orchard, as the gnarled trunks and low spreading branches would give the ideal setting to a house like this.

In the event of the house being built in a locality where field stone could easily be obtained, it would be advisable to use this material for the first story, as suggested in the illustration. The gables and roof are shingled and an admirable effect could be produced by using rived cypress shingles darkened by the application of diluted sulphuric acid. This brings out all the color in the wood and also brings it into complete harmony with the stone.

The porch at the front of the house is eight feet wide, permitting the use of a ham-

mock and such rustic furniture as is needed for veranda life in the summer. The second and smaller porch at the rear of the house opens into the dining room and may be used as an outdoor dining room during the warm months.

The vestibule inside the entrance door is very small, serving merely ·to cut off the draught from the door. This is one of our earlier plans and has narrower openings between the rooms. Were we to make it over now, we would suggest that the partition between the hall and the living room on the side

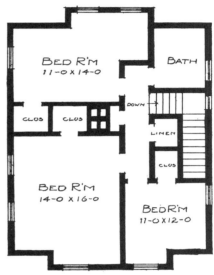

SECOND STORY FLOOR PLAN.

toward the front be taken away as far as the vestibule, making the hall a part of the living room. The narrow passage between the fireside seat and the staircase could remain unaltered, or the post-and-panel construction might be put across, making a doorway in which could be hung a portiére. Although the doorway between the living room and the dining room is very wide, yet the division is indicated sufficiently to separate the space into two distinct rooms. If this arrangement should be preferred, the opening could be left just as it is and either curtained with heavy portiéres, or partially filled with a large screen which could be spread across or removed at will. It would, however, be more in accordance with the later Craftsman arrangement to remove even these slight partitions, leaving only the chimneypiece to mark the division between the rooms.

FIRST STORY FLOOR PLAN.

Published in The Craftsman, December, 1908.

VIEW OF THE CLUBHOUSE AT CRAFTSMAN FARMS, SHOWING DECORATIVE EFFECT OF LOG CONSTRUCTION ON THE LOWER STORY AND THE PLASTER PANELS ABOVE. NOTE THE GROUPING OF THE WINDOWS AND THE DECORATED PANELS BETWEEN THE CASEMENTS IN THE DORMER. THE SLOPE OF THE HILL AT THE BACK SHOWS THE POSSIBILITY OF BUILDING THE BASEMENT ROOMS AS DESCRIBED.

A COUNTRY CLUBHOUSE THAT IS BUILT LIKE A LOG CABIN

WE have given the design of the Clubhouse at Craftsman Farms for the use of country clubs that may find such a plan desirable. As we use it ourselves, it will be the general assembly house of the whole colony, so planned that meals may be served either indoors or out on a big veranda, according to the weather, and where meetings, lectures and entertainments of all kinds may be held by the people staying at the Farms and accommodation provided for guests invited from the outside. For our own purpose, no form of building is so suitable and desirable as a low, roomy house built of logs, and we imagine that many a country club will find that similar uses and surroundings seem to demand a building of this character.

As will be seen by comparison of the exterior view of the house with the plan of the lower floor, there are three main divisions in the building, indicated in the perspective drawing by the projecting ends of the logs which form the log partition between the reception room and sitting room

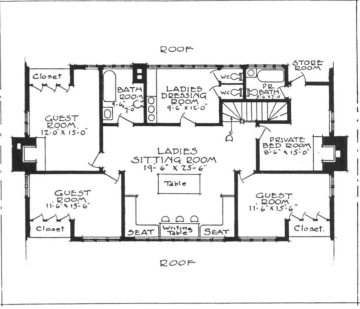

SECOND STORY FLOOR PLAN.

and kitchen on the one side, and serve as the outer wall of the house on the porch side. The width of this porch is the same as the width allowed for the sitting room and kitchen and the center of the building for the whole length is taken up by the reception room, which will be used for the assembly room or the indoor dining room, as seems necessary. The porch will be used as an outdoor living room or dining room, as the case may be, and the little sitting room at the back is meant for guests who may wish some place apart from the general assembly room for a quiet chat with a few friends.

The upper floor is divided into guest rooms, with a comfortable sitting room for ladies

FIRST STORY FLOOR PLAN.

79

A COUNTRY CLUBHOUSE

and a dressing room and two bathrooms, so that there is not only accommodation for transient guests but room for a few guests who may wish accommodation over night or for several days at a time.

The smoking room and dressing room for men are placed below the main floor, as in the case of the building at Craftsman Farms the ground slopes sufficiently away from the back of the house to allow ample accommodation for these basement rooms. This slope is sufficiently steep to expose the stone foundation to a depth of seven or eight feet, so that anyone entering the smoking room from the outside comes in on a level instead of going down as into a basement. Flower boxes placed between the pillars around this end of the porch will afford some protection where the slope is most abrupt.

As will be seen, the design of the house is very simple, the effect of comfort and of ample spaces depending entirely upon its proportions. The big sweep of the low pitched, widely overhanging roof is broken by the broad shallow dormers, which not only give sufficient additional height to make the greater part of the upper story habitable, but also adds much to the structural charm of the

building. As the walls of the upper story are of plaster, the logs being used after the manner of half-timber construction, the ends of the dormers are also of plaster and plaster panels divide the groups of casement windows.

These plaster panels form one of the most interesting features of the house because they put into effect our idea of a form of exterior decoration that shall be symbolic of the house itself and the environment in which it stands. Roughly modeled in low relief, are figures symbolizing the life and industries of the farm. Dull colored pigments will be used to emphasize these figures and to add a definite color accent to the house, but the pigments will in all cases come into harmony with the natural tones of wood, stone and earth. These panels form the sole decoration that exists purely for the sake of decoration. For the rest, the beauty of the house depends entirely upon structural features; upon the casement windows, which are all uniform in size and are so arranged as to form long horizontal lines; upon the use of the logs and of stone in the foundation and the chimneys and upon the color harmony of the whole in relation to the prevailing tones of the landscape.

UPSTAIRS SITTING ROOM, SHOWING THE WRITING TABLE AND SEATS IN THE DORMER.

A PLAIN LITTLE CABIN THAT WOULD MAKE A GOOD SUMMER HOME IN THE WOODS

Published in The Craftsman, November, 1908.

VIEW OF THE FRONT AND SIDE, SHOWING CASEMENTS HIGH IN THE WALL.

O NE of the features at Craftsman Farms is the housing of guests, students and workers in small bungalows or cabins scattered here and there through the woods and over the hillside, standing either singly or in groups of three and four in small clearings made in the natural woodland. Therefore they are designed especially for such surroundings and are most desirable for those who wish to build inexpensive summer or week-end cottages for holiday and vacation use. Of course, any one of the plans would serve perfectly well for a tiny cottage for two or three people to live in, but the design and general character of the buildings is hardly adapted to the ordinary town lot and would not be so effective in conventional surroundings as in the open country.

The cottages built at Craftsman Farms are meant first of all to live in and next to serve as examples of a variety of practical plans for small moderately priced dwellings designed on the general order of the bungalow. They will be built of stone, brick, or any one of a number of our native woods suitable for such construction and will be as comfortable, beautiful and interesting as we can make them, each one being specially planned for its own use.

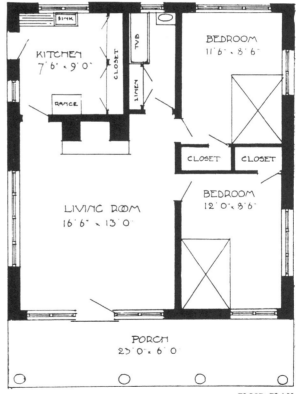

FLOOR PLAN.

Published in *The Craftsman, July, 1904.*

A BUNGALOW BUILT AROUND A COURTYARD FACING THE WATER: VIEW OF THE FRONT, SHOWING ENTRANCE, TERRACE AND CHIMNEYS, AND THE RELATION OF THE HOUSE TO ITS SITE.

A BUNGALOW BUILT AROUND A COURTYARD FACING THE WATER

O NE of our earliest designs is shown in this bungalow, which has proven very popular for summer homes, especially where they are built on the shore of a lake or river; for the chief characteristic of the design is an inner court, or *patio*, which looks directly out upon the water. The bungalow is built around three sides of this courtyard,—an arrangement which carries with it a suggestion of the old Mission architecture of California.

The original design was for a house with shingled walls, but the construction is equally suitable for stone, brick, or concrete. The material chosen, of course, would depend entirely upon the locality and the taste of the owner. Were we designing it now, we would probably suggest concrete, as the form of the house, with its straight walls and simple lines, is well suited to this material, and also because this method of construction is comparatively inexpensive as well as substantial and durable. If the walls were finished with rough plaster or pebbledash surface, the effect would be admirable, especially for the woods, if a little dull green pigment were brushed on irregularly, giving a general tone of green that yet is not a solid smooth color.

The central court as shown here is paved with stone, but this would be only in case of stone or shingle construction. For either brick or concrete it would be best to pave the court with cement colored a dull red and marked off into squares. This has much the appearance of Welsh quarry tiles and is much less expensive. Provision has been made in the center of the court for a basin, in the middle of which a pile of rocks affords opportunity for a fountain or trickling cascade, while the pool furnishes an admirable place for the growth of aquatic plants. The court can either be paved clear up to the pool as shown in the picture, or the pavement may stop just outside the pillars, leaving the center of the courtyard for turf. In either case the *patio* is meant to be furnished for use as an outdoor living room, such as is so frequently seen in the courtyards

FLOOR PLAN.

of California houses. If the house is built for a camp in the woods, the pillars around this courtyard would best be made of peeled logs left in the natural shape and stained back to the color of the bark. For more conventional use, heavy round pillars of concrete or of wood painted white would naturally be used. These details, however, are always ruled by the locality, the materials used for building and the taste of the builder.

The arrangement of the interior is very simple, as from the entrance hall one turns toward the right into the living room, which occupies half the front of the building. Just back of the living room in the wing is the dining room and back of this again is the kitchen. Turning to the left from the hall, a small passage leads to one of the bedrooms, and the other two bedrooms and the bathroom occupy the whole length of the wing. All of these rooms open out upon a central court and all are lighted from the outside by casements set high in the wall. Fireplaces are plentiful, the chimneys being so arranged that one is allowed for each bedroom and one for the living room. This being almost opposite the dining room, or rather alcove, serves for that room as well.

VIEW OF THE COURTYARD LOOKING OUT UPON THE WATER. THIS MIGHT BE USED AS AN OUTDOOR LIVING ROOM AND FURNISHED WITH TEA TABLE, CHAIRS, HAMMOCKS AND RUGS. BEING SO COMPLETELY SHELTERED FROM THE WIND IT SHOULD MAKE A VERY PLEASANT AFTERNOON LOUNGING PLACE IN WARM WEATHER.

A RUSTIC CABIN THAT IS MEANT FOR A WEEK-END COTTAGE OR A VACATION HOME

Published in The Craftsman, November, 1908.

FRONT VIEW OF CABIN, SHOWING DECORATIVE USE OF TRUSS IN THE GABLE.

THIS is another example of the cottages built at Craftsman Farms and is somewhat larger than the stone cabin shown on page 81, as it contains a bathroom and a recessed porch which serves as an open air dining room, in addition to the living room, two bedrooms and kitchen provided in the smaller cottage.

The walls are sheathed with boards eight or ten inches wide and seven-eighths of an inch thick. A truss of hewn timber in each gable, projecting a foot and a half from the face of the wall, not only gives added support to the roof, but forms a decorative feature that relieves the extreme simplicity of the construction. The casement windows are all hung so they will swing outward and are mostly small and set rather high in the wall. At the ends of the building these casements are protected by simple shutters, each one

made of two wide boards with either heart shaped or circular piercing. These solid shutters provide ample shelter in severe weather.

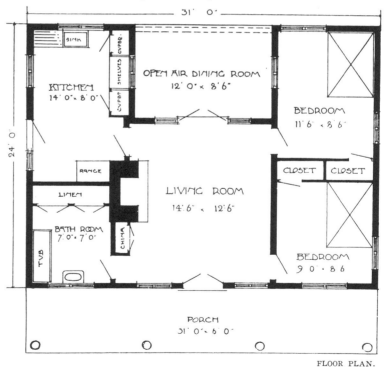

FLOOR PLAN.

A BUNGALOW DESIGNED FOR A MOUNTAIN CAMP OR SUMMER HOME

Published in The Craftsman, March, 1905.

REAR VIEW OF BUNGALOW, WITH VERANDA LOOKING TOWARD THE WATER.

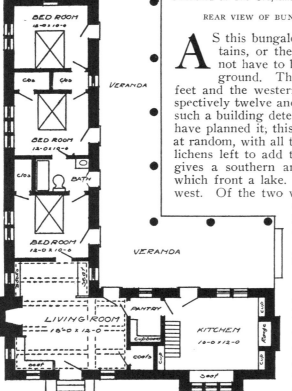

FLOOR PLAN.

AS this bungalow is meant either for the woods, the mountains, or the open country, where the cost of land does not have to be considered, it spreads over a good deal of ground. The eastern wing has a frontage of sixty-four feet and the western of forty-four feet, the verandas being respectively twelve and ten feet. Also the probable environment of such a building determines the character of the exterior. As we have planned it; this bungalow is built of rugged field stones set at random, with all the weather stains and accretions of moss and lichens left to add to the color value. The site suggested here gives a southern and western exposure to the wide verandas which front a lake. The building itself faces toward the northwest. Of the two wings, the eastern, containing the bedrooms, extends into the wooded portion of the land in order to insure protection and coolness; while the west wing looks toward the lake.

The interior of this bungalow is divided into a living room, a kitchen and three bedrooms. The living room is large and comfortably arranged, the idea being to give it a character in harmony with the plan, purpose and exterior effect of the building.

The kitchen is planned so that meals may be served in it in bad weather. Ordinarily the meals would be served in the sheltered corner of the veranda. The whole eastern wing is given up to the bedrooms which are all entered from the veranda, and overhead is a large storage attic.

86

A MOUNTAIN CAMP OR SUMMER HOME

FRONT VIEW OF BUNGALOW, SEEN FROM THE LAND.

CHIMNEYPIECE AND FIRESIDE NOOK IN THE LIVING ROOM. NOTE THE USE OF LOGS FOR OVERHEAD BEAMS AND OF WIDE V-JOINTED BOARDS FOR THE WALLS AND SEAT.

A CONVENIENT BUNGALOW WITH SEPARATE KITCHEN AND OPEN AIR DINING ROOM

Published in the Craftsman, April, 1906.

FRONT AND REAR VIEWS OF COTTAGE. THE FIRST SHOWING RECESSED ENTRANCE PORCH AND THE SECOND THE OPEN AIR DINING ROOM WHICH SEPARATES THE KITCHEN FROM THE MAIN PART OF THE HOUSE.

A BUNGALOW WITH OPEN-AIR DINING ROOM

OR any place, whether mountain or valley, that is really " in the country," the best form of summer home is the bungalow. It is a house reduced to its simplest form, where life may be carried on with the greatest amount of freedom and comfort and the least amount of effort. It never fails to harmonize with its surroundings, because its low broad proportions and absolute lack of ornamentation give it a character so natural and unaffected that it seems to sink into and blend with any landscape. It may be built of any local material and with the aid of such help as local workmen can afford, so it is never expensive unless elaborated out of all kinship with its real character of a primitive dwelling. It is beautiful, because it is planned and built to meet simple needs in the simplest and most direct way; and it is individual for the same reason, as no two families have tastes and needs alike.

The bungalow illustrated here is designed on the purest Craftsman lines. The material we have suggested is cedar shingles throughout with a foundation and chimney of rough gray stone. No cellar is provided, but the walls have a footing below the frost line and space under the floor for ventilation. The building is in the form of a T, the main portion covering a space twenty-four by forty feet and the extension at the back fourteen by thirty-six feet. The low-pitched, widely overhanging roof gives a settled, sheltered look to the building, and this is emphasized even more by the deeply recessed porch in front, which is meant to be used by a small outdoor sitting room. The porch be-

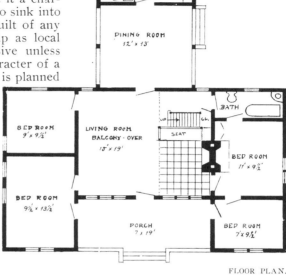

FLOOR PLAN.

tween the kitchen and the main part of the house is really a portion of the extension left with open sides and is intended for an outdoor dining room that shall be sufficiently sheltered

RECESSED ENTRANCE PORCH, SHOWING DOOR WITH THUMB LATCH AND HEAVY STRAP HINGES OF WROUGHT IRON; ALSO THE INTERESTING USE OF HEAVY TIMBERS IN THE DOOR AND WINDOW FRAMING, WHERE THE BEAM ACROSS THE TOP BINDS THE ENTIRE GROUP INTO A UNIT.

A BUNGALOW WITH OPEN-AIR DINING ROOM

END OF LIVING ROOM, SHOWING BALCONY, FIRESIDE NOOK WITH CHIMNEYPIECE AND ARRANGEMENT OF STAIRCASE.

ARRANGEMENT OF CUPBOARDS, WORK SHELF AND WINDOWS IN KITCHEN.

from storms to allow the outdoor life to go on through any sort of weather.

The living room occupies the whole center of the house, except for the recessed porch in front, and it is one of the best examples of the Craftsman idea of the decorative value that lies in revealing the actual construction of the building. Everyone knows the sense of space and freedom given by a ceiling that follows the line of the roof. It seems to add materially to the size of the room and when it is of wood it gives the keynote for a most friendly and restful color scheme. In this case the whole room is of wood, save for the rough gray plaster of the walls and the stone of the fireplace. A balcony runs across one side, serving the double purpose of recessing the fireplace

A BUNGALOW WITH OPEN-AIR DINING ROOM

OPEN-AIR DINING ROOM: NOTE CONSTRUCTION OF THE ROOF AND PROPORTION OF THE SIDE OPENINGS AND PARAPET.

into a comfortable and inviting nook, and of affording a small retreat which may be used as a study or lounging place, or as an extra sleeping place in case of an overflow of guests, or even as a storage place for trunks. Its uses are many, but its value as an addition to the beauty of the room is always the same.

The sleeping rooms, four in number, occupy the two ends of the main building. They are all of ample size for camp life, and are plastered, walls and ceiling. The dining porch is one of the most distinctive features of the bungalow. It occupies just half of the extension and completely separates the kitchen from the main part of the house. The kitchen is well open to air and light. Instead of a pantry the whole of one side is occupied by cupboards amply supplied with shelves and drawers.

AN OPEN FIRE IN ONE OF THE BEDROOMS.

A COTTAGE PLANNED WITH A SPECIAL IDEA TO ECONOMICAL HEATING

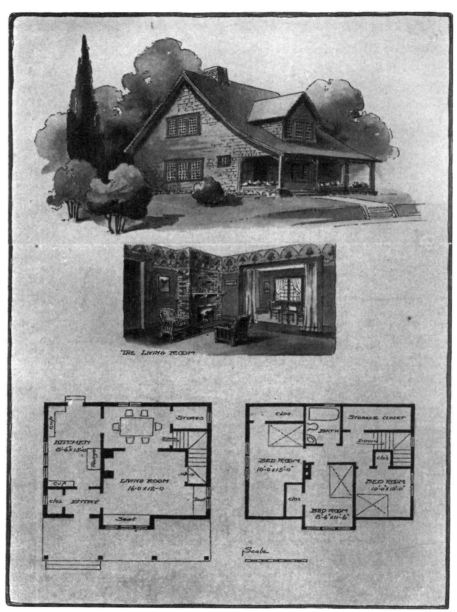

Published in The Craftsman, March, 1905.

NOTE THE USE OF THE BAY WINDOW ON THE LOWER FLOOR AND THE DORMER ABOVE TO ADD TO THE STRUCTURAL INTEREST OF THIS PLAIN LITTLE DWELLING. THE INTERIOR IS CAREFULLY PLANNED TO GIVE THE MOST CONVENIENT ARRANGEMENT OF ROOMS AND TO UTILIZE ALL THE SPACE, SO THAT THERE IS MORE ROOM IN THE HOUSE THAN MIGHT BE EXPECTED FROM THE SPACE OCCUPIED, WHICH IS THIRTY FEET FRONT BY TWENTY-TWO FEET DEEP.

A COTTAGE THAT COMES WITHIN THE LIMITS OF VERY MODERATE MEANS

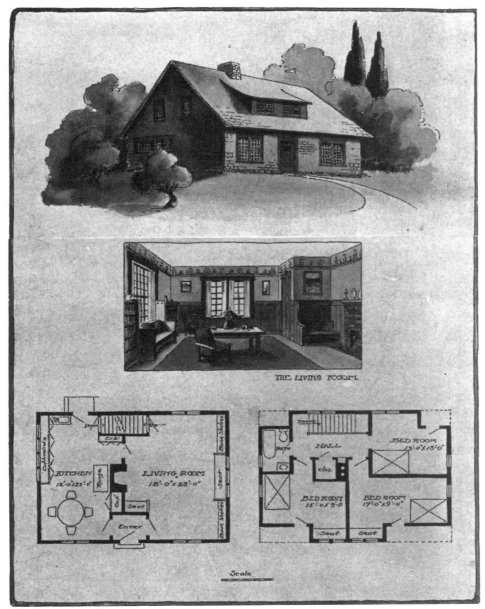

THE LIVING ROOM

Published in The Craftsman, March, 1905.

A COTTAGE WITH A FRONTAGE OF THIRTY-FOUR FEET AND A DEPTH OF TWENTY-FOUR FEET AND ARRANGED SO THAT THE ROOMS ARE A TRIFLE LARGER THAN THOSE IN THE COTTAGE SHOWN ON THE PRECEDING PAGE. AS NO SPACE IS TAKEN OFF FOR A VERANDA. THE COST OF THE TWO BUILDINGS IS ABOUT THE SAME AND COMES WITHIN VERY MODERATE MEANS.

Published in The Craftsman, July, 1903.

EXTERIOR VIEW OF MOUNTAIN CAMP, SHOWING RELATION TO SURROUNDINGS, USE OF ROUGH TIMBERS AND SLABS FOR CONSTRUCTION, WIDE OVERHANG OF ROOF AND DEEPLY RECESSED LOGGIAS FOR OUTDOOR SLEEPING ROOMS.

A COUNTRY HOUSE THAT WAS ORIGINALLY PLAN-
NED FOR A MOUNTAIN CAMP

ALTHOUGH this house would serve anywhere as a country dwelling for people who like this style of building, it was originally intended for a camp in the Adirondacks, the object of the design being to build a house that would be permanent, and at the same time would have the openness and freedom of a tent, where the family could live out of doors and yet have immunity from flies, mosquitoes and kindred pests. Being a camp, it is naturally not an expensive building, as the plan is simple and the materials about the site would naturally be used. Our constant dwelling upon this point might seem superfluous, but the fact that not long ago a noted architect built a house of stone in the clay-bearing State of Virginia and another of brick in the granite-ribbed State of Maine.

The word camp is suggestive, causing the mind instantly to revert to a large parade ground, with the orderly arrangement of kitchens in the rear, the radial axis, and the sense of order and openness. Therefore the arrangement of this camp has been made with this in mind; the great hall serves for the place of general gathering,—the place where, when the duties or pleasures of the day are over, all may meet on common ground. This, with the kitchen and dining room in the rear, makes for convenience, largeness and economy of

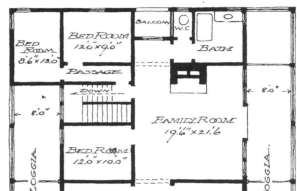

SECOND STORY FLOOR PLAN.

space. There is an upstairs; as sleeping rooms, if in direct connection with the rooms and arrangements already mentioned, would interfere and be interfered with seriously. Economy also has its part, for the roof which covers one story will serve equally well to cover two. In laying out the floors below, no account has been taken of privacy for the immediate family. Therefore on the upper floor there is a large room provided for with the sleeping rooms grouped about it.

The floor plans give a clear idea of the arrangement. The dropping back of the outside walls to form second story balconies or loggias takes up a good deal of the floor space on the second story, so that the bedrooms are rather small. This, however, is hardly to be considered a fault in a building of this kind, because the loggias are screened to serve as sleeping porches: It is also quite possible to screen or partition each loggia to make four separate outdoor sleeping rooms, or they could be divided in part and the rest used for an outside sitting room. These screens should be removable at will, so that they can be stored during the winter months.

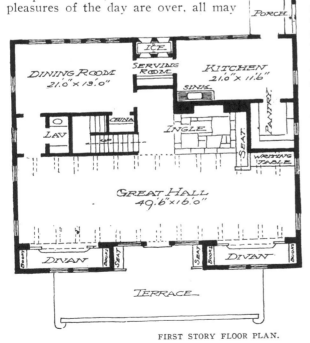

FIRST STORY FLOOR PLAN.

Published in The Craftsman, July, 1903.

GREAT HALL OF MOUNTAIN CAMP, SHOWING RECESSED FIREPLACE AND LONG FIRESIDE SEAT AND GIVING SOME IDEA OF THE WAY IN WHICH HEAVY TIMBERS ARE USED IN THE CONSTRUCTION.

PORCHES, PERGOLAS AND TERRACES: THE CHARM OF LIVING OUT OF DOORS

IN these days when the question of light and air is of so much importance in the planning of the home, the tendency is more and more toward the provision of ample room for as much open-air life as possible. In all the Craftsman houses, as well as in the best modern dwellings of other styles, the veranda, whether open in summer or enclosed for a sun room in winter, is one of the prominent features. Partly for convenience in enclosing with glass if desired, but mainly to insure the pleasant sense of privacy that means such a large part of the comfort of home, these porches or verandas are usually recessed so that they are partially protected by the walls of the house and are further sheltered by the copings and flower boxes. In a front porch which must serve for a sitting room as well as an entrance, the coping, surmounted by flower boxes, acts as a screen and, with the aid of a generous growth of vines, serves as a very satisfactory shelter from the street. Where there is also a garden veranda it can be made into a charming outdoor living or dining room both for summer and for mild days in winter by being so recessed and protected that it is like a summer house or an outdoor room always open to the sun and air.

Outdoor living and dining rooms, to be homelike and comfortable, should be equipped with all that is necessary for daily use so as to avoid the carrying back and forth of tables, chairs and the like, as when the veranda is used only occasionally. It goes without saying that the furniture should be plain and substantial, fitted for the rugged outdoor life and able to stand the weather. Indian rugs or Navajo blankets lend a touch of comfort and cheer, and the simple designs and primitive colors harmonize as well with trees and vines and the open sky as they do with their native wigwams. Willow chairs and settles seem to belong naturally to life in the garden, and with a few light tables, a book rack or two and plenty of hammocks, the veranda has all the sense of peace and permanency that should belong to a living room, whether indoors or out, that is habitually used by the family.

Published in The Craftsman, June, 1905.

COURTYARD AND PERGOLA, SHOWING DECORATIVE EFFECT OF THE CENTRAL SQUARE OF TURF WITH ITS FOUNTAIN, SHRUBS AND ROCKS AND THE COMFORT OF THE VINE-SHADED PORCH WHEN FURNISHED FOR USE AS AN OUTDOOR LIVING ROOM.

PORCHES, PERGOLAS AND TERRACES

Published in The Craftsman, November, 1906.

PORCH THAT NOT ONLY SERVES AS A DESIRABLE ENTRANCE BUT GREATLY INCREASES THE STRUCTURAL INTEREST OF THE FRONT OF THE HOUSE. THE WINDOWS ON EITHER SIDE PROJECT SLIGHTLY FROM THE WALL IN A SHALLOW BAY AND THE ENTRANCE DOOR WITH ITS CASEMENTS ON EITHER SIDE PROJECTS STILL FARTHER. THE PORCH IS COMPARATIVELY NARROW AND THE ROOF IS SUPPORTED BY TWO HEAVY PILLARS OF WOOD PAINTED WHITE, WHICH SERVE TO GIVE ACCENT TO THE DARKER TONES OF THE SHINGLES, EXTERIOR WOODWORK AND STONE FOUNDATION. THE WALLS ARE SHEATHED WITH CYPRESS SHINGLES THAT ARE OILED AND LEFT TO WEATHER, AND THE WOODWORK OF THE ROOF, DOOR AND WINDOW FRAMINGS AND BALUSTRADE IS IN A DARKER TONE OF BROWN. THE USE OF SPINDLES FOR EXTERIOR WOODWORK IS SHOWN IN THE BALUSTRADE.

PORCHES, PERGOLAS AND TERRACES

Published in The Craftsman, September, 1906.

ENTRANCE PORCH FITTED UP FOR AN OUTDOOR LIVING ROOM. FLOOR OF WELSH QUARRIES COVERED WITH A LARGE RUG INTENDED TO STAND ROUGH USAGE AND EXPOSURE TO THE WEATHER. THE BEAMED CEILING IS FORMED BY THE EXPOSED RAFTERS AND THE PORCH IS PARTIALLY SHELTERED BY THE PARAPET.

PORCHES, PERGOLAS AND TERRACES

Published in The Craftsman, May, 1906.

ENTRANCE PORCH TO A HOUSE BUILT OF ROUGH CAST CEMENT. THE WOODEN PILLARS ARE PAINTED PURE WHITE AND ARE VERY THICK AND MASSIVE IN PROPORTION TO THEIR HEIGHT. THE RAFTERS ARE LEFT IN VIEW WHERE THEY SUPPORT THE ROOF AND A HEAVY BEAM RUNNING THE LENGTH OF THE PORCH SERVES TO UPHOLD THE RAFTERS. SQUARE MASSIVE CROSS-BEAMS EXTEND FROM THE PILLARS TO THE WALL, WHERE THE ENDS ARE SUNK IN THE FRAMING OF THE HOUSE. THE FLOOR AND STEPS ARE OF CEMENT COLORED A DARK RED AND MARKED OFF IN BLOCKS LIKE TILES.

PORCHES, PERGOLAS AND TERRACES

Published in The Craftsman, November, 1904.

RECESSED PORCH AT REAR OF HOUSE, SHOWING RELATION OF THE PORTION THAT IS SHELTERED TO THE OPEN TERRACE THAT EXTENDS BEYOND THE ROOF AND GIVES SUFFICIENT SPACE FOR AN OUTDOOR LIVING ROOM THAT IS PARTLY OPEN TO THE SKY.

Published in The Craftsman, August, 1905.

RECESSED ENTRANCE PORCH FURNISHED AS AN OUTDOOR LIVING ROOM THAT IS PARTLY SHELTERED BY THE WALLS AND PARTLY SCREENED BY VINES.

THE EFFECTIVE USE OF COBBLESTONES AS A LINK BETWEEN HOUSE AND LANDSCAPE

IN the building of modern country homes there seems to be no end to the adaptability of cobblestones and boulders in connection with the sturdier kinds of building material, for, if rightly placed with regard to the structure and the surroundings, they can be brought into harmony with nearly every style of architecture that has about it any semblance of ruggedness, especially if the surrounding country be hilly and uneven in contour and blessed—or cursed—with a plentiful crop of stones.

effect of a loose pile of stones. Very few houses that are possible for modern civilized life,—outside of the mountain camp—are sufficiently rough and primitive in construction to be exactly in harmony with the use of cobbles, and always there is a slight sense of effort when they are brought into close relation with finished structure.

Nevertheless the popularity of cobblestones and boulders for foundations, pillars, chimneys and even for such interior use as chimney-pieces, is unquestioned and in many cases the

Published in The Craftsman, November, 1908, Hunt & Eager, Architects.

CEMENT PAVED TERRACE OF A CALIFORNIA HOUSE, SHOWING EFFECT OF COBBLESTONES IN WALLS AND PILLARS, AND THE WAY THEY HARMONIZE WITH THE ROUGH SHINGLE AND TIMBER CONSTRUCTION.

We have never specially advocated the use of cobblestones in the building of Craftsman houses, for as a rule we have found that the best effects from a structural point of view can be obtained by using the split stones instead of the smaller round cobbles. Splitting the stone brings into prominence all the interesting colors that are to be found in field rubble and it is astonishing what a variety and richness of coloring is revealed when the stone is split apart so that the inner markings appear. Also a better structural line can be obtained when foundation and pillars are clearly defined instead of having somewhat the

effect is very interesting. There is growing up in this country, especially on the Pacific Coast, a style of house that seems to come naturally into harmony with this sort of stone work, and there is no denying that when the big rough stones and cobbles are used with taste and discrimination, they not only give great interest to the construction, but serve to connect the building very closely with the surrounding landscape.

The fact that we have found the best examples of this natural use of boulders and cobbles in California seems to be due largely to the influence of Japanese architecture over

THE EFFECTIVE USE OF COBBLESTONES

Published in The Craftsman, November, 1908, Hunt & Eager, Architects.

VERANDA AND TERRACE OF THE SAME HOUSE, GIVING A GOOD IDEA OF THE WAY COBBLESTONES MAY SERVE TO LINK THE HOUSE WITH THE SURROUNDING LANDSCAPE. THE EFFECT OF THE RUGGED FORM OF PILLARS AND PARAPET IN CONNECTION WITH THE SHINGLES OF THE WALL AND THE LACY FOLIAGE OF THE TREE IS ESPECIALLY STRIKING.

THE EFFECTIVE USE OF COBBLESTONES

Published in The Craftsman, July, 1907, Greene & Greene, Architects.

A CALIFORNIA HOUSE MODELED AFTER THE JAPANESE STYLE, WITH HIGH RE-
TAINING WALL IN WHICH THE USE OF COBBLESTONES HAS PROVEN ESPECIALLY
DECORATIVE.

danger of incongruity, and on the other hand the stone is usually employed in a way that brings the entire building into the closest relationship with its environment.

The cobblestones used for the houses of this kind are of varying sizes. To give the best effect they should be neither too small nor too large. Stones ranging from two and one half inches in diameter for the minimum size to six or seven inches in diameter for the maximum size are found to be most generally suitable. Such stones, which belong of course to the limestone variety, and are irregularly rounded, can usually be obtained without trouble in almost any locality where there are any stones at all, picked up from rocky pasture land or a dry creek bottom. The tendency of builders is to select the whitest stones and the most nearly round that are obtainable.

This, however, applies only to the regular cobblestone construction as we know it in the East. In California the designers are much more daring, for they are fond of using large mossy boulders in connection with both brick and cobbles. The effect of this is singularly interesting both in color and form, for the warm purplish

the new building art that is developing so rapidly in the West. In these buildings the use of stone in this form is as inevitable in its fitness as the grouping of rocks in a Japanese garden, for on the one hand the construction of the house itself is usually of a character that permits such a use of stone without

brown of the brick contrasts delightfully with the varying tones of the boulders covered with moss and lichen, and the soft natural grays and browns of the more or less primitive wood construction that is almost invariably used in connection with cobbles gives the general effect of a structure that

THE EFFECTIVE USE OF COBBLESTONES

Published in The Craftsman, April, 1908, Grosvenor Atterbury, Architect.

PERGOLA, PORCH AND ENTRANCE OF A COUNTRY HOUSE AT RIDGEFIELD, CONNECTICUT. THE FOUNDATION AND FIRST STORY OF THE HOUSE ARE OF FIELD RUBBLE SET IN CEMENT, AND THE SECOND STORY IS BUILT OF OVER-BURNED BRICK WITH HALF-TIMBER CONSTRUCTION, GIVING A DELIGHTFUL COLOR EFFECT. THE HOUSE AND GARDEN ARE SO LINKED TOGETHER THAT THE FIRST IMPRESSION IS THAT OF PERFECT HARMONY AND CLOSE RELATIONSHIP, AN IMPRESSION THAT IS GREATLY HEIGHTENED BY THE USE MADE OF THE LOCAL STONE.

THE EFFECTIVE USE OF COBBLESTONES

Published in The Craftsman, July, 1907, Greene & Greene, Architects.

CONSTRUCTION OF THE PERGOLA AND ESPLANADE LEADING TO THE ENTRANCE OF A CALIFORNIA HOUSE. NOTE THE COMBINATION OF LARGE MOSSY BOULDERS WITH HARD-BURNED CLINKER BRICK SET IRREGULARLY IN DARK MORTAR.

in the illustration on page 105, where hard-burned brick and natural wood are most effectively combined with big rugged boulders and the large round slabs of stone that serve as steps. These stones, by their very conformation, p r o c l a i m themselves as belonging to New England, and the manner in which they are used is as definitely Eastern as the construction of the California houses is Western.

The Western method is admirably illustrated in the three different views given of the California house that so strongly reflects the influence of Japanese architecture. Here, instead of sharp-edged granite, we have big comfortable looking boulders with all the edges and corners worn off during the ages when they have rolled about in the mountain torrents, and the way they are w e d g e d helter-skelter among the irregular, roughly laid bricks of the walls, pillars and chimneys is as far from the conventional use of stone as is a Japanese garden from our own trim walks and flower beds. Such a combination as in shown in these pictures almost demands the suggestion of Japanese architecture in the house itself, and yet the whole thing belongs entirely to California.

The harmony of this house with its surroundings will be understood when we say that it is situated on high ground overlooking the wild gorge of the Arroyo Seco and that the trees close to it are gnarled, hoary oaks, towering eucalyptus, widespreading cottonwoods, tall, slim poplars and sycamores.

has almost grown up out of the ground, so perfectly does it sink into the landscape around it.

The same effect is being sought more and more in the East by certain daring and progressive architects who, without regard to style and precedent, are building houses suited to the climate, the soil and the needs of life in this country. An excellent example of this is shown

THE EFFECTIVE USE OF COBBLESTONES

Published in The Craftsman, November, 1907.

A HOUSE NEAR PASADENA, CALIFORNIA, SHOWING THE STRIKING EFFECT GAINED BY THE USE OF COBBLESTONES AND BOULDERS IN THE FOUNDATION, CHIMNEY AND YARD WALL.

Published in The Craftsman, November, 1907.

A CALIFORNIA HOUSE WHERE THE USE OF COBBLESTONES IN THE STRUCTURE ITSELF IS REPEATED IN THE LOW PILLARS THAT MARK THE ENTRANCE OF WALK AND DRIVEWAY AND IN THE GARDEN WALL, THUS DRAWING CLOSER THE RELATIONSHIP BETWEEN HOUSE AND GROUND.

THE EFFECTIVE USE OF COBBLESTONES

Published in The Craftsman, July, 1907, Greene & Greene, Architects.

A HOUSE IN SOUTHERN CALIFORNIA THAT SHOWS STRONG TRACES OF JAPANESE INFLUENCE, AS EVIDENT IN THE USE OF COBBLESTONES AND BOULDERS IN COMBINATION WITH BRICK, AS IN THE STRUCTURE ITSELF.

Published in The Craftsman, July, 1907, Greene & Greene, Architects.

AN EXCELLENT EXAMPLE OF THE RIGHT USE OF COBBLES AND BOULDERS. ANOTHER VIEW OF THE SAME HOUSE, SHOWING THE WAY IN WHICH THE GRACEFUL LINE OF THE CHIMNEY RISES FROM THE WALL OF BRICK AND STONE, AND ALSO THE MANNER IN WHICH THE STONE IS CARRIED PART WAY UP THE CHIMNEY SO THAT IT SHOWS IRREGULARLY HERE AND THERE.

BEAUTIFUL GARDEN GATES : THE CHARM THAT IS ALWAYS FOUND IN AN INTERESTING APPROACH TO AN ENCLOSURE

FEW people realize how much depends upon the approach to any given place. A pleasant entrance that rouses the interest and conveys some impression of individuality seems an earnest of pleasant things to come and is always associated in the memory with the anticipation that came from that first impression. Especially is this true of a garden gate, which for most of us holds a suggestion of sentiment and poetry because it is in its own way a symbol; it leads out to greater spaces or inward to more intimate beauty. Even to the most prosaic it always holds something of a promise of the peaceful and pleasant place that lies within. Thus it seems right that a garden gate should have a charm and grace all its own; that it should be embowered with trailing vines and blooming flowers in summer time and should always hold forth the inviting suggestion of pleasure and welcome beyond.

The illustrations given here are all of very simple garden gateways that are made attractive by the method of construction, by the placing of vines and flowers or by some graceful conceit in outline and relation to the surroundings. The hooded gate shown on this page forms a charming link between garden and garden. One may rest a moment within its shade and it seems to bind together the two plots of green divided by the fence. The trellised arbor and archway which spans the flower walk in an English garden is illustrated here because of the charming suggestion it contains for making a division between two parts of the same garden. The "pergola gate" shown below is illustrated without the vines that are meant to clothe it, because we desire to give a clear idea of the construction. The finely planned proportions of the heavy timbers and the straight unornamented lines suggest an inspiration from Japan. The vine covered rustic arbor which arches over the walk leading to the entrance of the house beyond is hardly a garden gate, yet it comes within the same class because it furnishes a most attractive approach to house and garden.

Published in The Craftsman, June, 1908.

A HOODED GATEWAY LEADING FROM ONE GARDEN TO ANOTHER. NOTE INTERESTING CONSTRUCTION OF THE ROOF AND THE WAY THE IDEA IS CARRIED OUT IN THE GATE AND THE FENCE.

Courtesy of John Lane Company.

ARBOR AND FLOWER WALK IN AN ENGLISH GARDEN, AFFORDING NOT ONLY A PLEASANT SUMMER RETREAT BUT ALSO A MOST ATTRACTIVE VISTA THROUGH THE LARGE GROUNDS.

Published in The Craftsman, June, 1908.

GATE WITH PERGOLA CONSTRUCTION OVERHEAD MEANT TO SERVE AS A SUPPORT FOR CLIMBING VINES

110

Published in The Craftsman, March, 1907.

HOMEMADE RUSTIC ARBOR, COVERED WITH CLIMBING ROSES AND HONEYSUCKLE, PLACED AT THE ENTRANCE OF THE WALK LEADING TO THE FRONT DOOR. ONE SUCH STRUCTURAL FEATURE AS THIS WOULD SERVE AS THE CENTRAL POINT OF INTEREST IN AN ENTIRE GARDEN.

111

Published in The Craftsman, March, 1907.

A VERY SIMPLE RUSTIC GATEWAY MADE OF TWO UPRIGHTS WITH CROSS-PIECES THAT SERVE AS A SUPPORT FOR VINES, AND A PEAKED HOOD OF THE SAME CONSTRUCTION, THE FENCE AND GATE ARE ALSO OF RUSTIC CONSTRUCTION. SUCH AN ENTRANCE ADDS A TOUCH OF DIGNITY AS WELL AS PICTURESQUENESS TO THE SIMPLEST GARDEN.

THE NATURAL GARDEN: SOME THINGS THAT CAN BE DONE WHEN NATURE IS FOLLOWED INSTEAD OF THWARTED

MAKING a garden is not unlike building a home, because the first thing to be considered is the creation of that indefinable feeling of restfulness and harmony which alone makes for permanence. Therefore, in planning a garden that we mean to live with all our lives, it is best to let Nature alone just as far as possible, following her suggestions and helping her to carry out her plans by adjusting our own to them, rather than attempting to introduce a conventional element into the landscape.

We have already explained in detail the importance of building a house so that it becomes a part of its natural surroundings; of planning it so that its form harmonizes with the general contour of the site upon which it stands and also of the surrounding country, and of using local materials and natural colors, wherever it is possible, so that the house may be brought into the closest relationship with its natural surroundings. But no matter how well planned the house may be, or how completely in keeping with the country, the climate and the

life that is to be lived in it, the whole sense of home peace and comfort is gone if the garden is left to the mercy of the average gardener, whose chief ambition usually is to achieve trim walks, faultless flower-beds and neatly barbered shrubs, and whose appreciation of wild natural beauty is small.

To give a real sense of peace and satisfaction a garden must be a place in which we can wander and lounge, pick flowers at our will and invite our souls, and we can do none of these if we have the feeling that trees, shrubs and flowers were put there arbitrarily and according to a set, artificial pattern, instead of being allowed to grow up as Nature meant them to do. Therefore, knowing the vital importance of the right kind of garden to the general scheme, we have given here some examples of the natural treatment of moderate-sized grounds, trusting that they may be suggestive to home builders. The house shown in the illustrations was built by an artist out in a pasture lot and the garden that has been encouraged to grow up around it has more of the

Published in The Craftsman, January, 1908.

A HOME WHERE THE SURROUNDINGS HAVE BEEN LEFT AS NEARLY NATURAL AS POSSIBLE; THE DWELLING OF MR. FREDERICK STYMETZ LAMB.

113

Published in The Craftsman, June, 1908.

A FLIGHT OF STEPS WHICH HAVE BEEN CUT OUT FROM THE SIDE OF A HILL AND REINFORCED WITH **HEAVY BOARDS** **ROUNDED AT THE EDGE.** THE CURVING LINE OF THE STEPS, WHICH CONFORMS TO THE CONTOUR **OF THE HILL, AND** THE DRAPERY OF VINES AND NATURAL UNDERGROWTH THAT COVERS THE RUSTIC RAILING ON **EITHER SIDE GIVES** TO THIS APPROACH A RARE AND COMPELLING CHARM.

Published in The Craftsman, January, 1908.

AN EXAMPLE OF THE EFFECT PRODUCED BY THE LAVISH USE OF VINES UPON A HOUSE WHERE THEY NATURALLY BELONG. THE CONSTRUCTION OF COBBLESTONE AND ROUGH CEMENT SEEMS TO DEMAND JUST SUCH GRACIOUS DRAPERY TO BRING IT INTO STILL CLOSER RELATIONSHIP WITH ITS SURROUNDINGS.

115

Published in The Craftsman, January, 1908.

A GARDEN THAT HAS MUCH OF THE SIMPLE CHARM OF A PASTURE LOT. TREES ARE LEFT TO GROW ALMOST AS THEY WILL. ROCKS LIE ABOUT HERE AND THERE AS ON A HILLSIDE AND THE FLOWERS ARE OF THE RUGGED HARDY VARIETY THAT ARE QUITE AT HOME IN THIS CLIMATE.

THE NATURAL GARDEN

feeling of free woods and meadows than of a primly kept enclosure. The trees were thinned out just enough to allow plenty of air and sunshine and the sense of space that is so necessary, and, for the rest, were permitted to grow as they would. As Nature never makes a mistake in her groupings, the different varieties of trees fall into the picture in a way that could never be achieved by the most ingenious planting. Such shrubs and flowers as have been set out are of the more hardy varieties that belong to the climate and to the soil, and the vines that clamber over the low stone garden walls and curtain the walls of the house seem more to belong to the wild growths of the hillside than to have been planted by man. Where there is a path or a flight of steps the course of it is ruled by the contour of the ground so that the whole impression is that of Nature smoothed down in places and in others encouraged to do her very best.

These pictures, of course, are only suggestive, for in the very nature of things this kind of a garden cannot be made by rule, as no two places require or will admit the same treatment. The only way to obtain the effect desired is to cultivate the feeling of kinship with the open country and with growing things, and so to learn gradually to perceive the orig-

inal plan. After that, all that is needed is to let things alone so far as arrangement goes, and to work in harmony with the thing that already exists.

Most fortunate is the home builder who can set his house out in the open where there is plenty of meadowland around it and an abundance of trees. If the ground happens to be uneven and hilly, so much the better, for the gardener has then the best of all possible foundations to start from and, if he be wise, he will leave it much as it is, clearing out a little here and there, planting such flowers and shrubs as seem to belong to the picture and allowing the paths to take the directions that would naturally be given to footpaths across the meadows or through the woods,—paths which invariably follow the line of the least resistance and so adapt themselves perfectly to the contour of the ground.

In connection with these garden pictures we give several illustrations of the effect of an abundant growth of vines over the walls of the house and around its foundations, and also show in one picture the result that can be obtained by allowing a fast growing vine to form a leafy shade to the porch that is used as an outdoor living room. The lattice construction of the roof admits plenty of sunlight.

Published in The Craftsman, December, 1907.
VINE COVERED PORCH THAT IS USED AS AN OUTDOOR LIVING ROOM AND THAT SEEMS MORE A PART OF THE GARDEN THAN OF THE HOUSE.

Published in The Craftsman, March, 1907.

AN OPEN SUMMER HOUSE WITH QUAINT THATCHED ROOF THAT FORMS AN INEXPENSIVE BUT MOST PICTURESQUE FEATURE IN A LARGE GARDEN, AND ALSO SERVES AS A PLAYHOUSE FOR THE CHILDREN.

WHAT MAY BE DONE WITH WATER AND ROCKS IN A LITTLE GARDEN

WE have to acknowledge our indebtedness to the Japanese for more inspiration in matters of art and architecture than most of us can realize, and in no department of art is the realization of subtle beauty that lies in simple and unobtrusive things more valuable to us as home makers than the suggestions they give us as to the arrangement of our gardens. With our national impulsiveness, we are too apt to go a step beyond the inspiration and attempt direct imitation, which is a pity, because the inevitable failure that must necessarily attend such mistaken efforts will do more than anything else to discourage people with the idea of trying to have a Japanese garden. But if we once get the idea into our heads that the secret of the whole thing lies in the exquisite sense of proportion that enables a Japanese to produce the effect of a whole landscape within the compass of a small yard, there is some hope of our being able to do the same thing in our own country and in our own way.

Our idea of a garden usually includes a profusion of flowers and ambitious-looking shrubs, but the Japanese is less obvious. He loves flowers and has many of them, but the typical Japanese garden is made up chiefly of stones, ferns, dwarf trees and above all water. It may be only a little water,—a tiny, trickling stream not so large as that which would flow from a small garden hose. But, given this little stream, the Japanese gardener,—or the American gardener who once grasps the Japanese idea,—can do wonders. He can take that little stream, which represents an amount of water costing at the outside about three dollars a month, and can so direct it that it pours over piles of rocks in tiny cascades, forming pool after pool, and finally shaping its course through a miniature river into a clear little lake. If it is a strictly Japanese garden, both river and lake will be bridged and the stream will have as many windings as possible, to give a chance for a number of bridges. Also it will have temple lanterns of stone, bronze storks and perhaps a tiny image of Buddha.

But in the American garden we need none of these things, unless indeed we have space enough so that a portion of the grounds may be devoted to a genuine Japanese garden like the one shown in the illustrations. This indeed might have been picked up in Japan and transplanted bodily to America, for it is the garden of Mr. John S. Bradstreet, of Minneapolis, who is a lover of all things Japanese and has been in Japan many times. This garden occupies a space little more than one hundred feet in diameter, and yet the two illustrations we give are only glimpses of its varied charm. They are chosen chiefly because they illustrate the use that can be made of a small stream of water so placed that it trickles over a pile of rocks. The effect produced is that of a mountain glen, and so perfect are the proportions and so harmonious the arrangement that there is no sense of incongruity in the fact that the whole thing is on such a small scale.

Where people have only a small garden, say in the back yard of a city home or in some nook that can be spared from the front lawn, an experiment with the possibilities of rocks, ferns and a small stream of water would bring rich returns. We need no temple lanterns or images of Buddha in this country, but we do need the kind of garden that brings to our minds the recollection of mountain brooks, wooded ravines and still lakes, and while it takes much thought, care and training of one's power of observation and adjustment to get it, the question of space is not one that has to be considered, and the expense is almost nothing at all.

The thing to be most avoided is imitation either of the Japanese models from which we take the suggestion for our own little gardens or of the scenery of which they are intended to remind us. It is safest to regard such gardens merely as an endeavor on our part to create something that will call into life the emotion or memory we wish to perpetuate.

All these suggestions are for a small garden such as would naturally belong to a city or suburban house, but if such effects can be produced here in a corner and by artificial means, it is easy to imagine what could be done with large and naturally irregular grounds, say on a hillside, or where a natural brook wound its way through the garden, giving every opportunity for the picturesque effects that could be created by very simple treatment of the banks, by a bridge or a pool here and there and by a little adjustment of the rocks lying around.

119

A PART OF A JAPANESE GARDEN OWNED BY MR. JOHN S. BRADSTREET, OF MINNEAPOLIS. AN EXCELLENT EXAMPLE OF HOW ROCKS, DWARF TREES AND A TINY STREAM OF WATER MAY BE USED TO MAKE A HIGHLY DECORATIVE EFFECT.

120

ANOTHER PART OF MR. BRADSTREET'S GARDEN, SHOWING BRIDGES MADE OF WATER-WORN TEAKWOOD TAKEN FROM AN OLD JUNK. THE FOUNTAIN, PILE OF ROCKS AND DWARF TREES ARE SEEN FROM A DIFFERENT ANGLE.

EXAMPLE OF WHAT MAY BE DONE WITH A VERY SMALL SUPPLY OF WATER. THE POOL HERE IS FED SOLELY BY A TINY STREAM WHICH ISSUES FROM THE DRAGON'S MOUTH AND FORMS A SLENDER CASCADE OVER THE ROCKS.

REST HOUSE AND POOL IN MR. BRADSTREET'S JAPANESE GARDEN, SHOWING TEMPLE LANTERN, SMALL IMAGE OF BUDDHA AND THE EFFECT OF ROCKS AROUND THE MARGIN FRAMING THE AQUATIC PLANTS IN THE POOL.

Published in The Craftsman, October, 1904.

VIEW OF THE GARDEN ENTIRE, SHOWING WHAT A SMALL SPACE IN THE YARD IS OCCUPIED BY AN ARRANGEMENT WHICH GIVES THE AMAZ-
ING EFFECTS SHOWN IN THE PRECEDING ILLUSTRATIONS.

HALLS AND STAIRWAYS: THEIR IMPORTANCE IN THE GENERAL SCHEME OF A CRAFTSMAN HOUSE

WITH the general adoption of the simpler and more sensible ideas of house building that have come to the front in late years, the hall seems to be returning to its old-time dignity as one of the important rooms of the house. Instead of the small dark passageway, with just room enough for the hat tree and the stairs, that we have long been familiar with in American houses, we have now the large reception hall with its welcoming fireplace and comfortable furnishings,—as inviting a room as any in the house. There is even a suggestion of the "great hall of the castle," where in bygone days all indoor life centered, in the ever-increasing popularity of the plan which throws hall, living room and dining room into one large irregular room, divided only by the decorative post-and-panel construction that we so frequently use to indicate a partition, or by large screens that serve temporarily to shut off one part or another if privacy should be required. In this main room all guests are received, all the meals are served and the greater part of the family life is carried on. Even where this plan is not adopted and the rooms of the lower story are completely separated from one another, the large reception hall is still counted as one of the principal rooms of the house, and what used to be considered the entrance or stair hall is now either absent entirely or treated as a vestibule; generally curtained off from the reception hall or living room into which it opens in order to prevent drafts from the entrance door.

Whether it be a large or small reception hall, or an entrance only large enough for the stairs and the passageway from the front door to the other rooms in the house, the hall is always worthy of careful consideration as to structural features and color scheme, for it gives the first impression of the whole house. It is the preface to all the rest and in a well planned house it strikes the keynote of the whole scheme of interior decoration. Above all things, the hall ought to convey the suggestion of welcome and repose. In a cold climate, or if placed on the shady side of the house, it is worth any pains to have the hall well lighted and airy and the color scheme rich and warm. It is the first impression of a house that influences the visitor and the sight of a cheerless vista upon entering chills any appreciation of subsequent effects. With a sunny exposure, or in a country where heat has to be reckoned with for the greater part

Published in The Craftsman, January, 1906.

A TYPICAL CRAFTSMAN STAIRWAY WITH LANDING USED AS A STRUCTURAL FEATURE OF THE RECEPTION HALL. THIS IS AN EXCELLENT EXAMPLE OF THE POST-AND-PANEL CONSTRUCTION WHICH IS SO OFTEN USED TO INDICATE THE DIVISION BETWEEN TWO ROOMS.

Published in The Craftsman, November, 1906.

AN UPPER HALL WHICH IS FITTED UP FOR USE AS A SEWING ROOM, STUDY, OR PLAYROOM, ACCORDING TO THE USE FOR WHICH IT IS MOST NEEDED. SUCH AN UPSTAIRS RETREAT IS DELIGHTFUL IN A HOUSE WHERE THE ARRANGEMENT OF THE WHOLE LOWER STORY IS OPEN, AS IT AFFORDS A MORE OR LESS SECLUDED PLACE FOR WORK OR STUDY AND YET HAS THE FREEDOM AND AIRINESS OF A LARGE SPACE.

HALLS AND STAIRWAYS

of the year rather than cold, an effect of restful shadiness and coolness is quite as inviting in its way, although it is always safe to avoid a cold color scheme for a hall, as the suggestion it conveys is invariably repellent rather than welcoming.

In England the large hall designed for the general gathering place of the family is a feature in nearly every moderately large house, particularly in the country. These English halls are always roomy and comfortable and in many cases are both picturesque and sumptuous in effect, having a certain rich stateliness that seems to have descended in direct line from the great hall of old baronial days. In this country the hall is more apt to be a part of the living room, and, while quite as homelike and inviting. is simpler in style.

The illustration on page 125 shows the part of a Craftsman reception hall that contains the stairway. A small den or lounging room is

formed by the deep recess that appears at one side of the staircase, which is central in position and is completely masked, excepting the lower steps and the landing, by the post construction above the solid wainscot that surrounds it. This wainscot turns outward to the width of a single panel at either side of the stair, one sheltering the end of the seat built in at the right side and the other partially dividing off the recess to the left. So arranged, the staircase forms an important part of the decorative treatment of the room.

The second illustration shows an upstairs hall, which has somewhat the effect of a gallery, as it is open to the stairway except for a low balustrade. This nook in the upper hall takes the place of a sewing room or an upstairs sitting room, and is infinitely more attractive because of the freedom and openness of the arrangement. While not in any sense a separate room, it still allows a certain seclusion

Published in The Craftsman, January, 1906.

A STAIRWAY THAT RUNS DIRECTLY UP FROM THE LIVING ROOM AND IS USED AS A PART OF THE STRUCTURAL DECORATION. NOTE THE LAMP ON THE NEWEL POST WHICH GIVES LIGHT TO THE SEAT BELOW AND THE WAY IN WHICH THE WINDOW ON THE LANDING CARRIES OUT THE LINE OF THE UPPER WALL SPACE.

127

HALLS AND STAIRWAYS

RECEPTION HALL AND STAIRCASE WHERE THE LANDING PROJECTS INTO THE ROOM ALMOST DIRECTLY OPPOSITE THE ENTRANCE DOOR. THIS HALL IN MOST CRAFTSMAN HOUSES IS LITTLE MORE THAN A NOOK IN THE LIVING ROOM.

for anyone who wishes to read, work or study.

The third illustration shows another Craftsman reception hall in which the staircase is the prominent structural feature. The double casements light stair and landing and also add considerably to the light in the room. Just below the stair is a comfortable seat with the radiator hidden below, and a coat closet fills the space between the seat and the wall.

A larger hall that is emphatically a part of the living room is seen in the last illustration. Here there is no vestibule and the wide entrance door with the small square panes in the upper part belong to the structural decoration of the room. Additional light is given from the same side by the row of casements recessed to leave a wide ledge for plants. The ceiling is beamed and the whole construction of the room is satisfying, although interest at once centers upon the staircase as the prominent structural feature. This is in the center of the room and has a large square landing approached by three shallow steps. The stairs run up toward the right at the turn and the space between steps and ceiling is filled with slim square uprights, two on each step, which give the effect of a grille, very open and very decorative. Opposite the stair on the landing is a railing about the height of a wainscot with posts above. Treated in this manner, the staircase seems intended as much for beauty as for utility, and so fulfills its manifest destiny in the Craftsman decorative scheme.

In a small house there are often many considerations which prevent the use of the hall as a living room. Many people object to the draughts and waste of heat entailed by the open stairway and prefer a living room quite separate from the entrance to the house. In this case it is better to omit the reception hall and to have merely a small entrance hall, rather than the compromise that contains no possibility of comfort and yet is crammed with all the features that belong in the larger hall intended for general use. An entrance hall of this kind may be made very attractive and inviting by the wise selection of the woodwork and color scheme and by care in the designing of the stairway, which of course is the principal structural feature in any hall.

THE LIVING ROOM: ITS MANY USES AND THE POSSIBILITIES IT HAS FOR COMFORT AND BEAUTY

UNQUESTIONABLY the most important room in the house is the living room, and in a small or medium sized dwelling this room, with the addition of a small hall or vestibule and a well-planned kitchen, is all that is needed on the first floor. A large and simply furnished living room, where the business of home life may be carried on freely and with pleasure, may well occupy all the space that is ordinarily partitioned into small rooms conventionally planned to meet supposed requirements. It is the executive chamber of the household, where the family life centers and from which radiates that indefinable home influence that shapes at last the character of the nation and the age. In the living room of the home,

more than in almost any other place, is felt the influence of material things. It is a place where work is to be done and it is also the haven of rest for the worker. It is the place where children grow and thrive and gain their first impressions of life and of the world. It is the place to which a man comes home when his day's work is done and where he expects to find himself comfortable and at ease in surroundings that are in harmony with his daily life, thought and pursuits.

In creating a home atmosphere, the thing that pays and pays well is honesty. A house should be the outward and visible expression of the life, work and thought of its inmates. In its planning and furnishing, the station in life of its owner should be expressed in a

Published in The Craftsman, April, 1907.

CHIMNEYPIECE AND FIRESIDE SEATS IN A TYPICAL CRAFTSMAN LIVING ROOM. THE CHIMNEYPIECE IS PANELED WITH DULL-FINISHED GRUEBY TILES BANDED WITH WROUGHT IRON HELD IN PLACE BY COPPER RIVETS. THE FIREPLACE HOOD IS OF COPPER AND THE PANELING OF SEATS AND WAINSCOT IS IN FUMED OAK.

Published in The Craftsman, December, 1905.

A LIVING ROOM WHICH IS ALSO USED FOR LIBRARY AND WORK ROOM. NOTE THE WAY IN WHICH THE DESK WITH ITS DRAWERS AND PIGEON HOLES IS BUILT INTO THE WALL SO THAT IT FORMS A PART OF THE BOOKCASE. THE LONG ROW OF CASEMENTS WITH THE WINDOW SEAT BELOW NOT ONLY FLOODS THE ROOM WITH LIGHT BUT FORMS A DECORATIVE FEATURE OF THE CONSTRUCTION.

THE LIVING ROOM

Published in The Craftsman, December, 1905.

A FIRESIDE NOOK THAT IS DEEPLY RECESSED FROM THE LIVING ROOM. THE CEILING OF THE NOOK IS MUCH LOWER THAN THAT OF THE MAIN ROOM, GIVING AN EFFECT OF COMFORT THAT IS HARD TO OBTAIN IN ANY OTHER WAY.

dignified manner, not disguised. If servants cannot be afforded without too heavy a tax upon the family finances, build the house so that it is convenient to get along without them. It is astonishing how easy the care of a house can be made by the simple process of elimi- nating unnecessary things. The right kind of a home does not drag out all that there is in a man to keep it going, nor is the care of it too heavy a burden upon a woman. It should

be so planned that it meets, in the most straightforward manner, the actual require- ments of those who live in it, and so furnished that the work of keeping it in order is reduced to a minimum.

It is the first conception of a room that decides whether it is to be a failure or a suc- cess as a place to live in, for in this lies the character that is to be uniquely its own. In every house, however, modest, there can be a

Published in The Craftsman, December, 1905.

CORNER OF A LIVING ROOM THAT IS ALSO USED AS A WORK ROOM. THE PANELING ON EITHER SIDE OF THE CHIM- NEYPIECE EXTENDS TO THE CEILING SO THAT THE ENTIRE WALL SPACE IS LINED WITH WOOD.

Published in The Craftsman, July, 1906.

CHIMNEYPIECE IN A MODERATE SIZED LIVING ROOM WHERE THE WALL TREATMENT ALLOWS THE INTRODUCTION OF A SHADOWY LANDSCAPE FRIEZE. THIS BEING SO DEFINITELY DECORATIVE, THE WALL SPACES BELOW ARE LEFT ABSOLUTELY PLAIN AND THE STRUCTURAL FEATURES ARE ALSO SEVERELY SIMPLE IN CHARACTER.

THE LIVING ROOM

living room that shows an individuality possessed by no other, an individuality that is actually a part of the place, if the room be planned to meet the real needs of those who are to live in it and to turn to the best advantage the conditions surrounding it. These conditions are as many as there are rooms. The situation and surroundings of the plot of ground on which a house is built has much to do with the position of the living room in the plan of that house. As it is the principal room, it should have an exposure which insures plenty of sunlight for the greater part of the day and also the pleasantest outlook possible to the situation. Both of these considerations, as well as the best arrangement of wall spaces, govern the placing of the windows and of outside doors, which may open into the veranda, the sun room, or the garden.

The structural variations of the living room are endless, as they are dominated by the tastes and needs of each separate family. If

Published in The Craftsman, February, 1902.

A RECESSED WINDOW SEAT THAT WOULD SERVE FOR ANY ROOM IN THE HOUSE.

the room is to be a permanently satisfying place to live in, nothing short of the exercise of individual thought and care in its arrangement will give the result. But one thing must be kept in mind if the room is to be satisfactory as a whole, and that is, to provide a central point of interest around which the entire place is built, decorated and furnished, for it gives the keynote both as to structure and color scheme. It may be a well planned fireplace, either recessed or built in the ordinary manner, with fireside seats, bookcases,

Published in The Craftsman, October, 1905.

A RECESSED FIREPLACE NOOK IN A ROOM WHERE THE WOODWORK IS LIGHT AND FINE AND THE PANELED WALL SPACES ARE COVERED WITH SOME FABRIC SUCH AS SILK, CANVAS, OR JAPANESE GRASS CLOTH.

THE LIVING ROOM

Published in The Craftsman, February, 1907.

A CHARACTERISTIC CRAFTSMAN INTERIOR, SHOWING THE ENTRANCE HALL, STAIRCASE AND LANDING AND A PART OF THE LIVING ROOM. NOTE THE WAY IN WHICH THE LINE OF THE MANTEL SHELF IS CARRIED THE WHOLE LENGTH OF THE WALL BY THE TOPS OF THE BUILT-IN BOOKCASES AND HOW IT IS FINISHED BY THE BALUSTRADE OF THE STAIR LANDING. ALSO NOTE THE MANNER IN WHICH THE ENTRANCE HALL IS DIVIDED FROM THE LIVING ROOM SO THAT ITS SEPARATENESS IS INDICATED WITHOUT DESTROYING THE SENSE OF SPACE WHICH MEANS SO MUCH TO THE BEAUTY OF THE MAIN ROOM.

Published in The Craftsman, November, 1905.

BUILT-IN CHINA CLOSETS ON EITHER SIDE OF THE FIREPLACE IN A LIVING ROOM WHICH IS ALSO USED AS A DINING ROOM. BY A SLIGHT DIFFERENCE IN ARRANGEMENT THE CUPBOARDS ABOVE COULD BE MADE TO SERVE AS BOOKCASES AND THOSE BELOW AS STORAGE PLACES FOR PAPERS, MAGAZINES AND THE LIKE.

THE LIVING ROOM

cupboards, shelves, or high casement windows so arranged as to be an integral part of the structure. The chimneypiece strikes a rich color-note with its bricks or tiles and glowing copper hood, and the woodwork, wall spaces and decorative scheme are naturally brought into harmony with it. Or perhaps the dominant feature may be the staircase, with its broad landing and well-designed balustrade; or it may be a group of windows so placed that it makes possible just the right arrangement of the wall spaces and commands the best of the view. Or if living room and dining room are practically one, the main point of interest may be a sideboard, either built into a recess or, with its cupboards on either side and a row of casement windows above, occupying the entire end of the room.

Any commanding feature in the structure of the room itself will naturally take its place as this center of interest; if there are several, the question of relative importance will be easily settled, for there can be only one dominant point in a well planned room. The English thoroughly understand the importance of this and the charm of their houses depends largely upon the skilful arrangement of interesting structural features around one center of attention to which everything else is subordinate. Also the English understand the charm of the recess in a large room. Their feeling regarding it is well expressed by a prominent English architect of the new school who writes: "Many people have a feeling that there is a certain cosiness in a small room entirely unattainable in a large room; this is a mistake altogether; quite the reverse has been my experience, which is, that such a sense

Published in The Craftsman, April, 1907.

FIREPLACE IN A LIVING ROOM. THE SQUARE MASSIVE CHIMNEYPIECE IS BUILT OF HARD-BURNED RED BRICK LAID UP IN DARK MORTAR WITH WIDE JOINTS. THE MANTEL SHELF AS ILLUSTRATED HERE IS OF RED CEMENT, BUT A THICK OAK PLANK WOULD BE EQUALLY EFFECTIVE. THE HOOD IS OF COPPER AND THE FIREPLACE IS BANDED WITH WROUGHT IRON. THE PANELING ABOVE THE BOOKCASES GIVES AN INTERESTING DIVISION OF THE WALL SPACES.

THE LIVING ROOM

of cosiness as can be got in the recesses of a large room can never be attained in a small one. But if your big room is to be comfortable, it must have recesses. There is a great charm in a room broken up in plan, where that slight feeling of mystery is given to it which arises when you cannot see the whole room from any one place in which you are likely to sit; when there is always something around the corner."

Where it is possible, the structural features that actually exist in the framework should be shown and made ornamental, for a room that is structurally interesting and in which the woodwork and color scheme are good has a satisfying quality that is not dependent upon pictures or bric-a-brac and needs but little in the way of furnishings.

Only such furniture as is absolutely necessary should be permitted in such a room, and that should be simple in character and made to harmonize with the woodwork in color and finish. From first to last the room should be treated as a whole. Such furniture as is needed for constant use may be so placed that it leaves plenty of free space in the room and when once placed it should be left alone. Nothing so much disturbs the much desired home atmosphere as to make frequent changes in the disposition of the furniture so that the general aspect of the room is undergoing continual alteration. If the room is right in the first place, it cannot be as satisfactorily arranged in any other way. Everything in it should fall into place as if it had grown there before the room is pronounced complete.

Published in The Craftsman, January, 1906.

WINDOW SEAT IN A LIVING ROOM. THE GROUP OF WINDOWS WITH THE SEAT BELOW EXTENDS ACROSS THE ENTIRE END OF THE ROOM AND THE TWO ENDS OF THE SEAT ARE FORMED BY THE SMALL SQUARE BOOKCASES BUILT INTO THE CORNERS.

THE DINING ROOM AS A CENTER OF HOSPITALITY AND GOOD CHEER

NEXT to the living room the most important division of the lower floor of a house is the dining room. The living room is the gathering place of the household, the place for work as well as for pleasure and rest; but the dining room is the center of hospitality and good cheer, the place for in a carefully planned house the work of the household is made as easy as possible. Hence it goes without saying that the dining room should be placed in such relation to the kitchen that the work of serving meals goes on with no friction and with as few steps as possible. A noiseless and well fitted swing

Published in The Craftsman, January, 1906.

CRAFTSMAN DINING ROOM WITH SIDEBOARD BUILT INTO A RECESS AND SURMOUNTED BY FOUR CASEMENT WINDOWS. NOTE HOW THE GROUPING OF THE WINDOWS IS REPEATED AT THE END OF THE ROOM.

that should hold a special welcome for guests and home folk alike. Instead of being planned to fulfil manifold functions like the living room, it has one definite use and purpose and no disturbing element should be allowed to creep in.

In planning a dining room two considerations take equal rank,—convenience and cheerfulness. Convenience must come first, door serves as a complete bar against sounds and odors from the kitchen, even if the connection be direct. If a butler's pantry should be preferred for convenience in serving, it would naturally be placed between the kitchen and the dining room. Much time and many steps are saved also if the principal china cupboard is built in the wall between the dining room and kitchen or butler's pantry, with

THE DINING ROOM

Published in The Craftsman, October, 1905.

DINING ROOM WITH DISH CUPBOARD BUILT INTO THE WALL SO THAT THE DOORS ARE FLUSH WITH THE SURFACE. THE SIDEBOARD IN THIS CASE IS MOVABLE AND THE REMAINDER OF THE WALL SPACE BELOW THE FRIEZE IS TAKEN UP BY A PICTURE WINDOW IN WHICH ARE ACCENTED THE COLORS THAT PREVAIL IN THE DECORATION OF THE ROOM.

Published in The Craftsman, November, 1905.

RECESSED WINDOW AND SEAT IN A DINING ROOM. AN UNUSUALLY QUAINT EFFECT IS GIVEN BY THE SMALL LEADED PANES OF GLASS AND THE BROAD WINDOW LEDGE FOR HOLDING PLANTS.

THE DINING ROOM

Published in The Craftsman, December, 1905.

SIDEBOARD BUILT INTO A RECESS WITH DISH CUPBOARDS ON EITHER SIDE. SQUARE MATT-FINISHED TILES ARE USED TO FILL IN THE PANELS ABOVE THESE CUPBOARDS AND THE SPACE BETWEEN THE TOP OF THE SIDEBOARD AND THE WINDOW LEDGE.

Published in The Craftsman, November, 1905.

WINDOW EXTENDING THE WHOLE WIDTH OF A DINING ROOM AND INTENDED FOR AN EXPOSURE WHERE THERE IS AN ESPECIALLY FINE VIEW.

THE DINING ROOM

doors opening on both sides so that dishes may be put away after washing without the necessity of carrying them into the dining room. Such an arrangement results in a great saving of broken china as well as in added convenience. This kind of a china cupboard may be made very decorative by putting small-paned or leaded glass doors on the dining room side and treating the wooden doors at the back like the wood trim of the room, which makes an effective setting for the china.

of cheerfulness may be given by the warmth of color in the room. A richness and decision of wall coloring that would grow wearisome in a room lived in all the time has all the pleasant and enlivening effects of a change when seen occasionally in a dining room. If the dining room is to be a part of the living room, it is well to plan it as one would a large recess. In that case the color scheme should, of course, be in close harmony with that of the living room; but even then it may strike a stronger

Published in The Craftsman, November, 1905.

ANOTHER FORM OF BUILT-IN SIDEBOARD WITH LINEN DRAWERS ON EITHER SIDE. THIS IS INTENDED TO FILL THE WHOLE SPACE ACROSS THE END OF THE DINING ROOM.

If possible, the dining room should have an exposure that gives it plenty of light as well as air. The windows play such an important part in the decoration of a room that a pleasant outlook is greatly to be desired. The brilliance of a sunny exposure may always be tempered by a cool and restful color scheme in walls and woodwork. On the other hand, if the room has a shady exposure and threatens to be somber on dark days, an atmosphere

and more vivid note in the walls, while the woodwork remains uniform throughout. A large screen placed in the opening of the recess may be made very decorative if it serve as a link in the color scheme as well as the leading element in that pleasant little sense of mystery that always accompanies a glimpse of something partially unseen.

Nowhere more than in the dining room is evidenced the value of structural features.

140

THE DINING ROOM

Almost all the decorative quality of the room depends upon them. In addition to wainscot and ceiling beams,—or instead of them if the room be differently planned,—the charm of well placed windows, large and small; of built-in cupboards, sideboards and cabinets for choice treasures of rare china or cut glass; of shelves and plate rack; of window ledge and window seat; and above all of a big cheery fireplace, is as never-ending as the ingenuity which gives to each really beautiful room exactly what it needs. And always it should be remembered that, in the dining room as in the living room, there should be one central structural feature which dominates all the rest.

Some examples of these ruling features are given in the accompanying illustrations. In one there is the wide sideboard built into a recess surmounted by three casement windows and flanked by a small china cupboard on either side. In another a wide window is recessed, giving a broad ledge for the growing things that always add beauty and life to a room. Still another recessed window shows a row of small-paned casements with plant ledge and a well cushioned seat below.

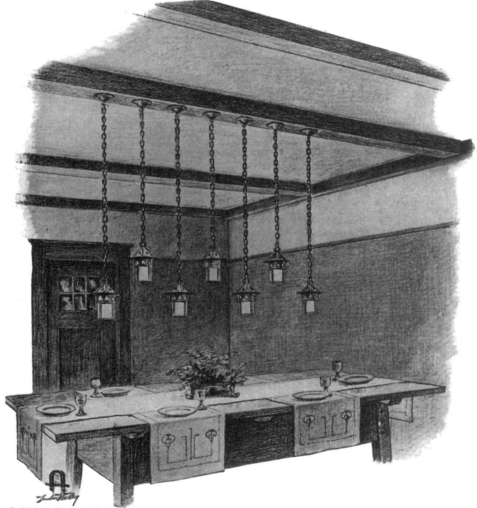

Published in The Craftsman, July, 1906.

A GROUP OF CRAFTSMAN SHOWER LIGHTS SWINGING FROM A BEAM OVER A LONG DINING TABLE. THIS IS ONE OF THE MOST EFFECTIVE METHODS WE HAVE FOUND OF MANAGING THE LIGHTS IN A DINING ROOM.

A CONVENIENT AND WELL-EQUIPPED KITCHEN THAT SIMPLIFIES THE HOUSEWORK

EACH room in the house has its distinct and separate function in the domestic economy. Therefore it should be remembered that before any room can attain its own distinctive individuality everything put into it must be there for some reason and must serve a definite purpose in the life that is to be lived and the work that is to be done in that room. Take for example the kitchen, where the food for the household must be prepared and where a large part of the work of the house must be done. This is the room where the housewife or the servant maid must be for the greater part of her

good fortune to associate such a room with their earliest recollections of home. No child ever lived who could resist the attraction of such a room, for a child has, in all its purity, the primitive instinct for living that ruled the simpler and more wholesome customs of other days. In these times of more elaborate surroundings the home life of the family is hidden behind a screen and the tendency is to belittle that part of the household work by regarding it as a necessary evil. Even in a small house the tendency too often is to make the kitchen the dump heap of the whole household, a place in which to do what cooking and

Published in The Craftsman, September, 1905.

CORNER OF THE KITCHEN SHOWING BUILT-IN CUPBOARD AND SINK.

time day after day, and the very first requisites are that it should be large enough for comfort, well ventilated and full of sunshine, and that the equipment for the work that is to be done should be ample, of good quality and, above all, intelligently selected. We all know the pleasure of working with good tools and in congenial surroundings; no more things than are necessary should be tolerated in the kitchen and no fewer should be required.

We cannot imagine a more homelike room than the old New England kitchen, the special realm of the housewife and the living room of the whole family. Its spotless cleanliness and homely cheer are remembered as long as life lasts by men and women who have had the

dishwashing must be done and to get out of as soon as possible. In such a house there is invariably a small, cheap and often stuffy dining room, as cramped and comfortless as the kitchen and yet regarded as an absolute necessity in the household economy. Such an arrangement is the result of sacrificing the old-time comfort for a false idea of elegance and its natural consequence is the loss of both.

In the farmhouse and the cottage of the workingman, where the domestic machinery is comparatively simple, cheerful and homelike, the kitchen,—which is also the dining room of the family and one of its pleasantest gathering places,—should be restored to all its old-time comfort and convenience. In

A CONVENIENT AND WELL-EQUIPPED KITCHEN

planning such a house it should come in for the first thought instead of the last and its use as a dining room as well as a kitchen should be carefully considered. The hooded range should be so devised that all odors of cooking are carried off and the arrangement and ventilation should be such that this is one of the best aired and sunniest of all the rooms in the house.

Where social relations and the demands of a more complex life make it impossible for the house mistress to do her own work and the kitchen is necessarily more separated from the rest of the household, it may easily be planned to meet the requirements of the case without losing any of its comfort, convenience, or suitability for the work that is to be done in it. Modern science has made the task very easy by the provision of electric lights, open plumbing, laundry conveniences, and hot and cold running water, so that the luxuries of the properly arranged modern kitchen would have been almost unbelievable a generation ago. Even if the kitchen is for the servant only, it should be a place in which she may take some personal pride. It is hardly going too far to say that the solution of the problem of the properly arranged kitchen would come near to being the solution also of the domestic problem.

The properly planned kitchen should be as open as possible to prevent the accumulation of dirt. Without the customary "glory holes" that sink and other closets often become, gen-

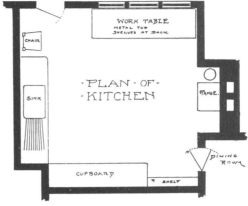

FLOOR PLAN.

uine cleanliness is much easier to preserve and the appearance of outside order is not at all lessened. In no part of the house does the good old saying, "a place for everything and everything in its place," apply with more force than in the kitchen. Ample cupboard space for all china should be provided near the sink to do away with unnecessary handling and the same cupboard, which should be an actual structural feature of the kitchen, should contain drawers for table linen, cutlery and smaller utensils, as well as a broad shelf which provides a convenient place for serving. The floor should be of cement and the same material may be used in tiled pattern for a high wainscot, giving a cleanly and pleasant effect.

Published in The Craftsman, September, 1905.

RANGE SET IN A RECESS TO BE OUT OF THE WAY AND WORK TABLE PLACED JUST BELOW A GROUP OF WINDOWS.

THE TREATMENT OF WALL SPACES SO THAT A ROOM IS IN ITSELF COMPLETE AND SATISFYING

SO much of the success of any scheme of interior decoration or furnishing depends upon the right treatment of the wall spaces that we deem it best to take up this subject more in detail than it has been possible to do in the general descriptions of the houses or even of the separate rooms.

It goes without saying that we like the friendly presence of much wood and are very

practical value in the life of the household, as such furnishings mean great convenience, economy of space and the doing away with many pieces of furniture which might otherwise be really needed, but which might give the appearance of crowding that is so disturbing to the restfulness of a room.

When the walls are rightly treated, it is amazing how little furniture and how few or-

Published in The Craftsman, October, 1904.

A HIGH WAINSCOT MADE WITH RECESSES TO HOLD CHOICE BITS OF METAL OR EARTHENWARE. THIS IS ESPECIALLY BEAUTIFUL IF CARRIED OUT IN CHESTNUT OR GUMWOOD TREATED IN THE CRAFTSMAN MANNER.

sensible of the charm of beams, wainscots and built-in furnishings which are a part of the house itself and so serve to link it closer to the needs of daily life. Bare wall spaces, or those covered with pictures and draperies which are put there merely for the purpose of covering them, are very hard to live with. But wall spaces that provide bookcases, cupboards, built-in seats for windows, fireside and other nooks are used in a way that not only gives to them the kind of beauty and interest which is theirs by right, but makes them of

naments and pictures are required to make a room seem comfortable and homelike. The treatment of wall spaces in itself may seem but a detail, yet it is the keynote not only of the whole character of the house but of the people who live in it. We hear much criticism of the changing and remodeling which is deemed necessary every year or two because a house must be "brought up to date" or because the owners "grow so tired of seeing one thing all the time." Yet both of these reasons are absolutely valid so far as they go, for the

THE TREATMENT OF WALL SPACES

majority of houses are in themselves so uninteresting that it is little wonder that the people who live in them have always a sense of restlessness and discontent, and that they are always doing something different in the hope that eventually they may find the thing which satisfies them.

We believe that the time to put thought into the decoration of a home is when we first begin to draw up the plans, and that the first consideration in each room should be the adjustment of the wall spaces so that there is not a foot of barren or ill-proportioned space in the entire room. It is true that utility and the limitations of the plan are necessarily the first considerations; that the ceilings of all the rooms on one story must be of uniform height in a house where the expense of construction is a thing to be considered; that windows must be placed where they will admit the most light and that doors are meant to serve as means of communication between rooms or with the outer world. Yet working strictly within these limitations, it is quite possible to adjust the height of each room so

Published in The Craftsman, June, 1905.
WALL DIVIDED INTO PANELS BY STRIPS OF WOOD.

that, no matter what may be its floor space, to all appearances its proportions are entirely harmonious; to place doors and windows so that, instead of being mere holes in the wall, they become a part of the whole structural scheme, and to see that in shape and proportions as well as in position they come into entire harmony with the rest of the room.

Published in The Craftsman, October, 1907.

LOW WAINSCOT WITH BROAD PANELS. NOTE THE PLACING OF THE WINDOW SO THAT IT REALLY FORMS A DECORATIVE PANEL IN THE WALL SPACE ABOVE.

THE TREATMENT OF WALL SPACES

Published in The Craftsman, June, 1905.
ATTRACTIVE TREATMENT OF WALLS IN A BEDROOM OR WOMAN'S SITTING ROOM.

Naturally, in considering the treatment of the wall spaces, the most important feature is the woodwork, especially if the room is to be wainscoted. Where this is possible, we would always recommend it, particularly for the living rooms of a house, as no other treatment of the walls gives such a sense of friendliness, mellowness and permanence as does a generous quantity of woodwork. The larger illustra-

tions reproduced here give some idea of what we mean and of what may be done with wall spaces when it is possible to use much wood in the shape of wainscot and beams. It will be noted that in each case the wall is of the same height; yet owing to the treatment of the spaces, each one appears to be different. Also note the way in which windows, doors and fireplace form an integral part of the structural scheme and how they are balanced by the wall spaces around them so that the whole effect is rather that of a well planned scheme of structural decoration than of the introduction of a purely utilitarian feature.

When we speak of the friendliness of woodwork, however, we mean woodwork that is so finished that the friendly quality is apparent, —which is never the case when it is painted or stained in some solid color that is foreign to the wood itself, or is given a smooth glassy polish that reflects the light. When this is done the peculiar quality of woodiness, upon which all the charm of interior woodwork depends, is entirely destroyed and any other material might as well be used in the place of it. In a later chapter we purpose to deal more

Published in The Craftsman, October, 1907.
TREATMENT OF WAINSCOTED WALL IN A LIVING ROOM WHERE THE PANELING IS REPEATED IN THE FRIEZE AND THE FIREPLACE IS PERFECTLY PROPORTIONED IN RELATION TO THE WALL SPACES ON EITHER SIDE.

THE TREATMENT OF WALL SPACES

fully with the question of finishing interior woodwork so that all its natural qualities of color, texture and grain are brought out by a process which ripens and mellows the wood as if by age without changing its character at all. Here it is sufficient to say that any of our native woods that have open texture, strong grain and decided figure,—such as oak, chestnut, cypress, ash, elm or the redwood so much used on the Pacific coast,—are entirely suitable for the woodwork of rooms in general use, and that each one of them may be so finished that its inherent color quality is brought out and its surface made pleasantly smooth without sacrificing the woody quality that comes from frankly revealing its natural texture.

The first illustration (page 144) shows a wainscot that is peculiarly Craftsman in design. The panels are very broad and what would be the stiles in ordinary paneling are even broader. At the top of each panel is a niche in which may be set some choice bit of pottery or metal work that is shown to the best advantage by the wood behind it and that serves to give the accents or high lights to the whole color scheme of the room. The

Published in The Craftsman, June, 1905.

TREATMENT OF PLAIN WALLS WITH LANDSCAPE FRIEZE.

wall space above is of plain sand-finished plaster that may either be left in the natural gray or treated with a coat of shellac or wax which carries the color desired. The rough texture of the plaster has the effect of seeming to radiate color, while it absorbs the light instead of reflecting it as from a smoothly polished surface, and when the color is put on lightly enough to be a trifle uneven instead of a dead solid hue without variation of any sort, there is a chance for the sparkle and play of light which at once adds life and interest.

Published in The Craftsman, October, 1907.

WALL WITH A HIGH WAINSCOT IN WHICH THE DOOR AND WINDOW ARE MADE A PART OF THE STRUCTURAL DECORATION: THE LEADED PANELS IN WINDOW AND DOOR ADD MUCH TO THE BEAUTY OF THE ROOM.

Published in The Craftsman, August, 1905.

TREATMENT OF WALLS IN A NURSERY. PLAIN ROUGH PLASTER BELOW AND A SHADOWY SUGGESTION OF A FOREST IN THE FRIEZE. BY THIS ARRANGEMENT THE SURFACE OF THE LOWER WALL IS EASILY KEPT CLEAN AND YET ALL APPEARANCE OF BARRENNESS IS AVOIDED.

Published in The Craftsman, August, 1905.

ANOTHER SUGGESTION FOR THE TREATMENT OF NURSERY WALLS, SHOWING A PICTURE DADO ILLUSTRATING NURSERY TALES AND A BLACKBOARD BUILT INTO THE WAINSCOT WITHIN EASY REACH OF THE LITTLE ONES.

FLOORS THAT COMPLETE THE DECORATIVE SCHEME OF A ROOM

ONE of the most important elements in the success of a room designed to be beautiful as a whole in structure and color scheme, is the floor. Whether it be a more or less elaborate parquet floor or one made simply of plain boards, it must be in harmony with the color chosen for the wood trim of the room. Also it should invariably be at least as dark as the woodwork, if the effect of restfulness is to be preserved. A floor that strikes a higher note of color than the woodwork above it, even if it be otherwise harmonious in tone, gives the room a top-heavy, glaring effect that no furniture or decoration will remove.

Full directions for finishing floors will be given later in the chapter on wood finishes. While the Craftsman method of finishing woodwork differs widely from others, it does not apply so much to the floor, for here a filler should be used for precisely the same reason that it should be avoided in the treatment of furniture and woodwork, as it destroys the texture of the wood by covering it with a glassy, smooth and impervious surface. Texture is not needed in the wood of a floor, which should be entirely smooth and non-absorbent.

The first of the three floors illustrated here is meant to complete the color scheme of a room in which the woodwork is of silver-gray maple and the furniture and decorations are in delicate tones such as would naturally harmonize with gray. The floor is very simple in design, having a plain center of silver-gray maple that is finished exactly like the woodwork of the room. Around the edge is a wide border of "mahajua," a beautiful Cuban hardwood, close and smooth in grain and left in its natural color, which is a greenish gray slightly darker than the finish of the maple.

The second floor is made of quartered oak in the natural color, and the boards are bound together with keys of vulcanized oak. Where the floor is stained to match the woodwork in tone, the color value of boards and keys will remain the same, as the vulcanized oak keys will simply show a darker shade of whatever color is given the boards of plain oak. The last illustration shows a floor of quartered oak in the natural color combined with vulcanized oak and white maple to form a border in which a primitive Indian design appears.

Published in The Craftsman, October, 1905.

A FLOOR OF SILVER-GRAY MAPLE AND MAHAJUA.

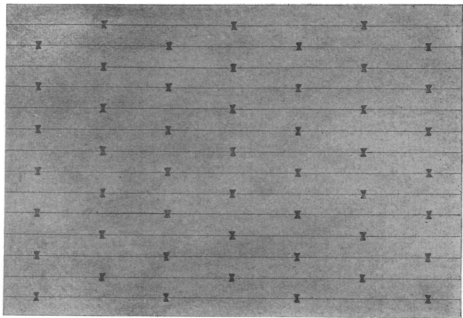

Published in The Craftsman, October, 1905.

FLOOR OF NATURAL OAK INLAID WITH KEYS OF VULCANIZED OAK.

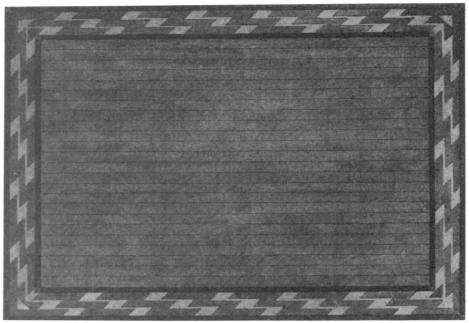

Published in The Craftsman, October, 1905.

FLOOR OF OAK INLAID WITH MAPLE. BORDER IN INDIAN DESIGN.

AN OUTLINE OF FURNITURE-MAKING IN THIS COUNTRY: SHOWING THE PLACE OF CRAFTSMAN FURNITURE IN THE EVOLUTION OF AN AMERICAN STYLE

THIS book is meant to give a comprehensive idea of the elements that go to make up the typical Craftsman home. Therefore at least one chapter must be devoted to Craftsman furniture, for in the making of this we first gave form to the idea of home building and furnishing which we have endeavored to set forth. For this reason, and because the furniture has so far remained the clearest concrete expression of the Craftsman idea, we are here illustrating a few of the most characteristic pieces that

scope of their experience, for, after the first primitive days of the Pilgrim Fathers in New England and the earliest settlers in the South, the life of the Colonists was modeled closely upon that of the old country and this life naturally found expression in their dwellings and household belongings. Therefore the Colonial style was so close to the prevailing style of the eighteenth century that it may be regarded as practically the same thing.

After the end of the Colonial period, and during the swift expansion that followed the

ONE OF THE LARGEST AND MOST MASSIVE OF THE CRAFTSMAN SETTLES; MADE OF FUMED OAK; SOFT LEATHER SEAT.

serve to show all the essential qualities of the style.

In order that the reader may understand clearly the reasons which led to the making of Craftsman furniture, and its place in the evolution of a distinctively American style that bids fair eventually to govern the great majority of our dwellings and household belongings, we will first briefly review the history of furniture making in this country. With the older styles, such as the English and the Dutch Colonial, we have little to do. They were importations from older civilizations, as were the Colonists themselves, and they expressed the life of the mother country rather than that of the new. When we first began to make furniture in this country, the cabinetmakers naturally followed their old traditions and made the kind of furniture which most appealed to them and which came within the

Revolution, there was inevitably a return to the primitive. Importations from the old world were no longer popular and while the houses of the wealthy were still furnished with the graceful spindle-legged mahogany pieces of earlier days, most of the people were forced to content themselves with much plainer and more substantial belongings. Little chair factories sprang up here and there, especially in Maine, Vermont and Massachusetts, and these supplied the great demand for the plain wooden chairs that we now call kitchen chairs, and the cane-seated chairs which were usually reserved for use in the best room. As the demand increased with the increasing population, the alert and resourceful New Englander began to invent machinery which would increase his output. As a consequence, the business of chair making made rapid growth, but the primitive

FURNITURE MAKING IN THIS COUNTRY

AN ARM-CHAIR AND ROCKER THAT ARE BUILT FOR SOLID COMFORT AS WELL AS DURABILITY.

beauty of the hand-made pieces was lost. The Windsor chairs, with their perfect proportions, subtle modeling and slender legs shaped with the turning lathe, became a thing of the past, for in the factories it was necessary from a business point of view to effect the utmost savings in material and also to consider the limitations of the machinery of that day. The object of the manufacturer naturally was to turn out the greatest possible quantity of goods with the least possible amount of labor and expense, and the result was so many modifications of the original form that the factory-made chairs soon become commonplace. When machines were invented to take the place of hand turning and carving, it was inevitable that vulgarity should be added to the commonplaceness, be-

LARGE CRAFTSMAN LOUNGING CHAIR.

cause it is so easy to disguise bad lines with cheap ornamentation.

Side by side with these chair factories another furniture industry was springing up, mainly in the Middle West because that was the black walnut country and black walnut was the material most in demand for the more elaborate furniture. At the same time that the New Englander was evolving from the artisan who carried on his work with the aid of a little water mill, to a manufacturer who owned a chair factory run by machinery, a number of German cabinetmakers who had settled in Indiana and the neighboring states were accumulating, by means of industry and thrift, enough means to set up general

LARGE OCTAGONAL TABLE, TOP COVERED WITH HARD LEATHER. DESIGNED FOR LIBRARY OR LIVING ROOM.

furniture factories, which supplied the country with black walnut "parlor suits," upholstered with haircloth, repps or plush, while the New Englander remained content to furnish it with dining room and kitchen chairs.

This period in our furniture corresponds with the architectural phase in this country which has aptly been termed the "reign of terror," but we are in some measure consoled for the hideous bad taste of it all by the reflection that it was contemporary with the early and mid-Victorian period in England, a term that everywhere stands for all that is ugly, artificial and commonplace in household art. It was succeeded by the first of the Grand Rapids furniture, which was in some measure a change for the better. Tempted by the success of the German furniture makers, the

FURNITURE MAKING IN THIS COUNTRY

shrewd New England manufacturers, with their superior knowledge of machinery, managed to plant themselves in t h e Middle West and to distance their competitors. The center of these new manufacturing interests was then in Grand Rapids, Michigan, so that the new style of furniture which was produced came to be k n o w n as G r a n d Rapids furniture. It was plainer than the black walnut furniture and was fashioned more after the Colonial models, but the best features were speedily lost in the ornamentation with which it was overlaid, as well as in the modification and adaptation of the earlier forms by a new generation of designers, who had studied foreign furniture and so gained a smattering of the traditional styles which they proceeded to apply to the creation of "novelties." About this time the large department stores sprang up and, as they very soon became the principal retailers, they naturally assumed control of the furniture that was made. The demand for novelties was unceasing and the designer was at the beck and call of the traveling salesman, who in his turn was compelled to supply a ceaseless stream of new attractions to the head of the furniture department,—whose business it was constantly to whet the public

LOW ROCKER AND DROP-LEAF SEWING TABLE WITH THREE DRAWERS; THE UPPER ONE HAVING A SLIDING TRAY MADE OF CEDAR WITH COMPARTMENTS FOR SPOOLS.

appetite for further novelties.

The greater part of the demand thus created was satisfied by the Grand Rapids f u r n i t u r e, but as wealth and culture increased, and people became more and more familiar with European homes and European luxuries. the new vogue for the "period" furniture sprang up among the richer c l a s s, and some of the factories turned their attention to endeavoring to duplicate the several styles of French and English furniture of the seventeenth and eighteenth centuries. These factories are still running, some of them being employed in turning out the closest imitation they can make of the "period" furniture and others in reproducing Colonial models.

While we were doing these things in America, Ruskin and Morris had been endeavoring to establish in England a return to handicrafts as a means of individual expression along the several lines of the fine and industrial arts. This gave rise over there to the Arts and Crafts movement, which was based chiefly upon the expression of untrammeled individualism. Much furniture was made,—some of it good, but a great deal of it showing the eccentricities of personal fancy un-

ROUND TABLE THAT IS WELL ADAPTED TO GENERAL USE.

CHESS OR CHECKER TABLE HAVING TOP COVERED WITH HARD LEATHER MARKED OFF INTO SQUARES FOR THE BOARD.

A BOOKCASE THAT IS A GOOD EXAMPLE OF THE DECORATIVE USE OF PURELY STRUCTURAL FEATURES.

permanent style in English furniture for the reason that they have striven for a definite and intentional expression of art that was largely for art's sake and had little to do with satisfying the plain needs of the people. Although the founders of the movement held and preached the doctrine that all vital art necessarily springs from the life of the people, it is nevertheless recognized even by their followers that in practice such expression as they advocate belongs to the artist alone and that the people care very little about it.

A LIGHT WRITING TABLE FOR A LIVING ROOM OR SMALL SITTING ROOM.

modified by any settled standards. It was a move in the right direction because it meant a return to healthy individual effort and a revolt from the dead level established by the machines. But the Arts and Crafts workers have not succeeded in establishing another

It was during this same period that the movement called *L'Art Nouveau* sprang up in France and for a time attained quite a vogue under the leadership of Bing. Belgium followed suit with a rather heavier and more pronounced interpretation of the distinctive features of this style and for a few years the plant forms and swirling lines that distinguished *L'Art Nouveau* productions were very popular. In Germany and Austria the art students and others of the more restless spirits who were constantly in revolt from the established styles determined to outdo the French and accordingly established government schools for the teaching of a definite style, which was called New Art or Secessionist and which

RUSH SEATED CHAIR AND DROP LEAF TABLE WITH SEPARATE WRITING CABINET.

contained some of the features of *L'Art Nouveau* and others that were borrowed from the English Arts and Crafts and also from ancient Egyptian forms of art. The French school has already failed in the efforts to establish a permanent style, and the indications are that the efforts of the German and Austrian Secessionists will prove equally futile, because in both cases the workers have merely attempted to do something different; to evolve a new thing by combining the features of the old. In other words, they began at the top instead of beginning at the bottom and allowing the style to develop naturally

A LARGE WRITING DESK FOR THE LIBRARY OR WORKROOM.

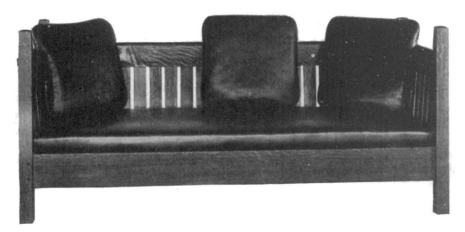

A TYPICAL CRAFTSMAN LOUNGING CHAIR.

from the sure foundation of real utility. The leaders succeeded in making things that, whatever their relative merits, were a new departure; but this once made, it stood as a completed achievement that might be imitated, but could hardly be developed, as it lacked the beginnings of healthy growth.

But during the same period in this country things were on a different basis. Out of the chaos of ideals and standards which had naturally resulted from the rapid growth of the young nation, a vigorous and coherent national spirit was being developed, and amid the general turmoil and restlessness attendant upon swift progress and expansion, it became apparent that we were evolving a type of people distinct from

A LARGE OAKEN SETTLE UPHOLSTERED WITH CRAFTSMAN SOFT LEATHER. THE PILLOWS ARE COVERED WITH THE STILL SOFTER AND MORE FLEXIBLE SHEEPSKIN.

FURNITURE MAKING IN THIS COUNTRY

all others,—a type essentially American. And the distinguishing characteristic of this type is the power to assimilate so swiftly the kind of culture which leads to the making of permanent standards of life and art that it is hardly to be compared with what might seem to be the corresponding class in other countries. Such Americans have fundamental intelligence and the power of discrimination, and the direct thinking that results from these qualities inevitably produces a certain openness of mind that responds very quickly to

ness alone. In this country, where we have no monarchs and no aristocracy, the life of the plain people is the life of the nation; therefore, the art of the age must necessarily be the art of the people. Our phases of imitation and of vulgar desire for show are only a part of the crudity of youth. We have not yet outgrown them and will not for many years; but as we grow older and begin to stand on our own feet and to cherish our own standards of life and of work and therefore of art, we show an unmistakable tendency to

A GROUP OF CRAFTSMAN SPINDLE FURNITURE. THIS IS QUITE AS STRONG AND DURABLE AS THE MORE MASSIVE PIECES BUT IS A LITTLE LIGHTER IN APPEARANCE.

anything which seems to have a real and permanent value.

This quality was shown in the immediate recognition and welcome accorded to Craftsman furniture when we first introduced it ten years ago. Like the Arts and Crafts furniture in England, it represented a revolt from the machine-made thing. But there was this difference: The Arts and Crafts furniture was primarily intended to be an expression of individuality, and the Craftsman furniture was founded on a return to the sturdy and primitive forms that were meant for useful-

get away from shams and to demand the real thing.

And to an American the real thing is something that he needs and understands. The showroom quality is all very well when it comes to proving how much money he has or to establishing a reputation for owning things that are just as good as his neighbor's. But for use he wants the things that belong to him,—the things that are comfortable to live with; that represent a good investment of his money and have no nonsense about them. Furthermore the true American likes to know how things are done. His interest and sympathy are immediately aroused when he sees something that he really likes and knows to be a good thing, if he is able to feel that, if he wanted it and had the time, he could make one like it himself.

So strong is this national characteristic that it is hardly overstating the case to say that in America any style in architecture or furniture would have to possess the essential qualities of simplicity, durability, comfort and convenience and to be made in such a way that

SMALL WRITING DESK FOR A WOMAN'S SITTING ROOM OR FOR THE LIVING ROOM

the details of its construction can be readily grasped, before it could hope to become permanent. We are not so many generations removed from our pioneer forefathers that we have grown entirely out of their way of getting at things. We may not always stop to think about them, but when we do our thought is apt to be fairly sound and direct. The prevalence of cheap, showy, machine-made things in our houses is due chiefly to the lack of thought that

A BIG DEEP CHAIR THAT MEANS COMFORT TO A TIRED MAN WHEN HE COMES HOME AFTER THE DAY'S WORK.

takes on trust the word of the dealers, and every year brings us more abundant proof that they do not in any way represent the real tastes and standards of the people. All machine-made imitations of furniture which belonged to another country and another age and represented the life of a totally different people, are alike to the average American. If he can get them cheap, he has at least the satisfaction of feeling that they make a pretty good outward show for the money; if they are expensive, there is something in being able to afford them and to know that his house has in it rooms which are fairly

NO BETTER EXAMPLES OF THE CRAFTSMAN STYLE CAN BE FOUND THAN ARE SHOWN IN THIS CHAIR AND ROCKER.

FURNITURE MAKING IN THIS COUNTRY

successful imitations of the rooms in French or English palaces two or three hundred years ago. But in all this there is no real thought and nothing that approaches it. It is only when a thing has the honest primitive quality that reveals just what it is, how it is made and what it is made for, that it comes home to us as something which possesses an individuality of its own. It is not an elaborate finished thing made by machinery with intricate processes which we cannot understand and about which we do not care in the least; it is something that we might make with our own hands. Therefore it is something that sets us to thinking and establishes a point of contact from which springs the essentially human qualities of interest and affection. Understanding just how it is made, we are in a position to appreciate exactly what the artisan has done and how well he has done it. From this understanding comes the personal interest in good work that alone gives the vital quality which we know as art.

Many people misunderstand the meaning of the word primitiveness, mistaking it for crudeness, but the word is used here to express the directness of a thing that is radical instead of derived. In our understanding of the term, the primitive form of construction is that which would naturally suggest itself to a workman as embodying the main essentials of a piece of furniture, of which the first is the straightforward provision for practical need. Also we hold that the structural idea should be made prominent because lines which clearly define their purpose appeal to the mind with the same force as does a clear concise statement of fact. This principle is the basis from which the Craftsman style of furniture has been developed. In the beginning there was no thought of creating a new style, only a recognition of the fact that we should have in our homes something better suited to our needs and

FURNITURE MAKING IN THIS COUNTRY

SERVING TABLE AND TWO OF THE LIGHTER DINING CHAIRS, SUITABLE FOR A DINING ROOM TOO SMALL TO TAKE THE MORE MASSIVE FURNITURE: UPHOLSTERED WITH LEATHER.

more expressive of our character as a people than imitations of the traditional styles, and a conviction that the best way to get something better was to go directly back to plain principles of construction and apply them to the making of simple, strong, comfortable furniture that would meet adequately everything that could be required of it.

Because Craftsman furniture expresses so clearly the fundamental sturdiness and directness of the true American point of view, it follows that in no other country and under no other conditions could it have been produced at the present day. The history of art shows us that a new form of expression never develops from the top and that nothing permanent is ever built upon tradition. When a style is found to be original and vital it is a certainty that it has sprung from the needs of the plain people and that it is based upon the simplest and most direct principles of construction. This is always the beginning and a style that has in it sufficient vitality to endure, will grow naturally as one worker after another feels that he has something further to express. In making Craftsman furniture we went back to the beginning,

seeking the inspiration of the same law of direct answer to need that animated the craftsmen of an earlier day, for it was suggested by the primitive human necessity of the common folk. It is absolutely plain and unornamented, the severity of the style marking a point of departure from which we believe that a rational development of the decorative idea will ultimately take place.

LARGE SIDEBOARD THAT IS USUALLY MADE IN OAK FINISHED IN A VERY LIGHT TONE OF BROWN, WITH PULLS AND HINGES IN DULL, BROWNISH COPPER, FORMING A DECORATIVE EFFECT.

159

WILLOW CHAIRS AND SETTLES WHICH HARMONIZE WITH THE MORE SEVERE AND MASSIVE FURNITURE MADE OF OAK

AN ARM CHAIR OF WOVEN WILLOW.

THE opinion is frequently expressed with regard to Craftsman furniture that it is all very well for the library, den or dining room, but that an entire house furnished with it would be apt to appear too severe and monotonous in its general effect. While naturally we feel that Craftsman furniture is equally suitable for every room in the house, we are aware that there is precisely the same element of truth in this criticism that it holds when applied to any kind of furniture. The point is that too much of any one thing is apt to be monotonous, and the way we avoid that fault in a Craftsman house is to make the furniture entirely a secondary thing and keep it as little obtrusive as possible, so that each piece sinks into its place in the picture and becomes merely a part of the general impression, instead of standing out as a separate article.

In the Craftsman houses we do away with a great deal of the movable furniture by the use in its place of built-in fittings, which are made a part of the structure of the house. As these include window seats, fireside seats, settles, bookcases, desks, sideboards, china cupboards and many other things, it will easily be seen that their presence not only adds to the structural interest and beauty of the room itself, but makes it possible to dispense with much of the furniture which would otherwise be needed. For the rest, we use Craftsman furniture where it is necessary to have pieces of wood construction, but we relieve any possible severity of effect by a liberal use of willow settles and chairs which afford the best possible foil to the austere lines, massive forms and sober coloring of the oak. We select willow for this use rather than rattan, because, while all such furniture is necessarily handmade, the rattan pieces are usually patterned after the elaborate effects that we have learned to associate with machine-made goods, and so have none of the natural interest that is a part of something which grows under the hand and is shaped as simply as possible to meet the purpose for which it is intended.

The charm of willow is that it is purely a handicraft, and obviously so. A rattan chair or settle may be twisted into any fan-

A HIGH-BACK SETTLE OF WILLOW THAT HARMONIZES ADMIRABLY WITH THE GENERAL CHARACTER OF CRAFTSMAN FURNITURE.

WILLOW CHAIRS AND SETTLES

tastic form, but willow furniture is essentially of basket construction. Our idea in making the kind of willow furniture illustrated here was to gain something based upon the same principles of construction that characterize our oak furniture; that is, to secure a form that should suggest the simplest basket work and the flexibility of lithe willow branches and yet be as durable as any of the heavy oak furniture which is emphatically of wood construction.

Consequently these pieces are basketry pure and simple and have an elastic spring under the pressure of the body that suggests the flexibility of baskets such as are woven by the fireside or on the back porch at the edge of the garden. The making of willow furniture as a handicraft is rather a hobby with us, for willow is a material beloved of the craftsman and the work is very interesting and comparatively easy to do. The trouble is that so many people are inclined to overdo it and to make out of woven willow the kind of furniture that demands wood construction. Seat furniture alone is permissible in willow and yet we frequently see tables, racks and stands of various kinds, and even the front of a bureau or a dresser, made of this material. Such misuse is a pity, the more that it tends to create a prejudice again against willow furniture as a whole.

The pieces shown here hold in their beauty of form and color evidences of the personal interest of the worker. The willow has been so finished that the surface has the sparkle seen in the thin branches of the growing tree as it becomes lustrous with the first stirring of the sap. This natural sparkle on the surface of willow has all

WILLOW CHAIR MADE ON A LOWER AND BROADER MODEL.

the intangible silvery shimmer of water in moonlight. This is lost absolutely when the furniture made of it is covered with the usual opaque enamel, which not only hides the luster of the surface but gives the effect of a stiff uncompromising construction in which the pliableness of the basket weave is entirely obliterated and all the possible interesting variations of tone are lost under the smooth surface.

We finish our willow furniture in two colors; one gives the general impression of green, but it is really a variation of soft wood tones, brown and green, light and dark, as the texture of the withes has been smooth or rough. In this way the silvery luster of the willow is left undisturbed and the color beneath is like that of fresh young bark. The other color is golden brown in which there is also a suggestion of spring-like gray and green.

VERY LARGE WILLOW SETTLE MADE AFTER A DESIGN THAT WE HAVE FOUND MOST SATISFACTORY IN RELATION TO THE REGULAR CRAFTSMAN FURNITURE OF OAK.

CRAFTSMAN METAL WORK: DESIGNED AND MADE ACCORDING TO THE SAME PRINCIPLES THAT RULE THE FURNITURE

IN a room decorated according to Craftsman ideas,—especially if it be furnished with Craftsman furniture,—it is of the utmost importance that the metal accessories should be of a character that fits into the picture. We found out very soon after we began to make the plain oak furniture that even the best of the usual machine-made and highly polished metal trim was absurdly out of place, and that in order to get the right thing it was necessary to establish a metal-work department in the Craftsman Workshops where articles of wrought metal in plain rugged designs and possessing the same structural and simple quality as the furniture could be made. We began with such simple and necessary things as drawer and door pulls, hinges and escutcheons, but with a work so interesting and so full of possibilities as this one thing inevitably leads to another, and our metal workers were soon making in hand-wrought iron, copper and brass all kinds of household fittings, such as lighting fixtures, fire sets, and other articles that were decorative as well as

LARGE LANTERN THAT IS BEST FITTED FOR USE IN AN ENTRANCE HALL OR VERANDA.

useful, and that showed the same essential qualities as the furniture.

Since then we have not only made all manner of metal furnishings ourselves, but through the pages of THE CRAFTSMAN we have warmly encouraged amateur workers to do the same thing and have given for their use a number of models as well as full directions regarding methods of working and the necessary equipment for doing all kinds of simple metal work at home. Under the inspiration of these suggestions and directions, a number of readers of THE CRAFTSMAN have set up little home workshops and have succeeded in making many pieces that show originality and merit. In fact, metal work is one of the most interesting of the crafts to the home worker who possesses skill and taste and, above all, a genuine interest in making for himself the things that are needed either for use or ornament at home, and anyone who takes it up and discovers its possibilities is likely to go on with it indefinitely. Instruction in the technicalities is easily obtained from any blacksmith who can teach the rudiments of handling iron, or from any working jeweler or coppersmith who is able to give the necessary personal supervision to the first efforts of a worker in brass or copper. Given even a little ingenuity and handiness with tools, it

COPPER-FRAMED LANTERN THAT IS INTENDED TO HANG FROM A BRACKET ATTACHED TO THE WALL.

CRAFTSMAN METAL WORK

might be possible to dispense even with this instruction and to work out each problem as it comes up; learning by doing, in the simple way of the handicraftsman of old.

It ought to be possible for such home workers to make everything necessary for the fireplace, including shovels and tongs, andirons, fenders, coal buckets and even fireplace hoods, although the last named might be a fairly ambitious undertaking for an amateur. One needs but little imagination to realize the interest and charm that would attach to a comfortable fireside nook that had been furnished in this way, and the same principle applies to every one of the smaller articles of furniture in the home. For example, it is not at all hard to make from either brass or copper a tray or an umbrella stand, a simple vase or metal jug or a jardiniére, and the decorative quality of such things is really wonderful; that is, if the worker takes care to confine himself to simple good designs that meet as directly as possible the need for which the article is made, and then makes it just as well as he can, keeping free from the temptation so commonly common to metal workers of artificially heightening the "hand-wrought" effect by putting hammer dents where they have no business to be, leaving the edges rough and generally exaggerating into crudity the traces of workmanship which, if rightly used, give to a piece such a human interest and charm. Much of the effect depends upon the way the metal is finished. For example, all of our wrought-iron work is finished in a way that has

SMALL SQUARE LANTERN MEANT TO HANG FROM THE CEILING OR AN OVERHEAD BEAM.

SQUARE LANTERN WITH AN UNUSUALLY DECORATIVE COPPER FRAME.

ELECTROLIER IN FUMED OAK AND HAMMERED COPPER, ESPECIALLY DESIGNED FOR HANGING RATHER LOW OVER A DINING TABLE.

ONE OF THE LITTLE LANTERNS THAT IS FREQUENTLY USED WITH THE SHOWER LIGHTS.

ELECTRIC LANTERN DESIGNED AS A FINIAL TO A NEWEL POST.

long been known in England as "armor bright." This is a very old process used by the English armorers, whence it derives its name, and its peculiar value is that it finishes the surface is a way that brings out all the black, gray and silvery tones that naturally belong to iron, and also prevents it from rusting. This method applies to both wrought iron and sheet iron and is the only thing we know that accomplishes the desired result. The process itself is very simple. After the iron is hammered it should be polished on an emery belt; or if this is not at hand and it is not convenient to borrow the use of one in some thoroughly equipped metal shop, emery

CRAFTSMAN METAL WORK

cloth—about Number O—may be used in polishing the surface by hand.

Then the iron must be smoked over a forge or in a fireplace, care being taken to avoid heating it to any extent during this process, as the object is merely to smoke it thoroughly. It should then be allowed to cool naturally and the surface rubbed well with a soft cloth dipped in oil. Naturally, the more the iron is polished the brighter it will be, especially in the higher parts of an uneven surface, which take on almost the look of dull silver. After this the piece must be well wiped off so that the oil is thoroughly removed, and the surface lacquered with a special iron lacquer.

To give the copper the deep mellow brownish glow that brings it into such perfect harmony with the fumed oak, the finished piece should be rubbed thoroughly with a soft cloth dipped in powdered pumice stone, and then left to age naturally. If a darker tone is desired, it should be held over a fire or torch and heated until the right color appears. Care should be taken that it is not heated too long, as copper under too great heat is apt to turn black. We use no lacquer on either copper or brass, age and exposure being the only agents required to produce beauty and variety of tone. All our brass work is made of the natural unfinished metal, which has a beautiful greenish tone and a soft dull surface that harmonizes admirably with the natural wood. Like copper, it darkens and mellows with age.

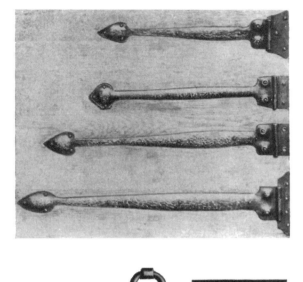

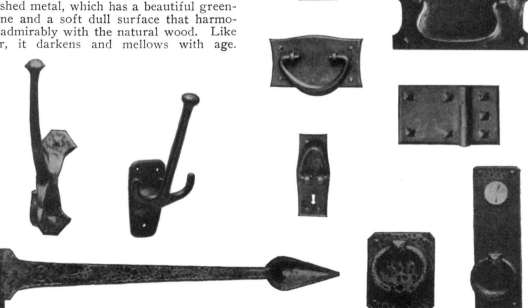

CHARACTERISTIC CRAFTSMAN HINGES, DOOR AND DRAWER PULLS, KNOCKERS AND COAT HOOKS, ALL DESIGNED TO HARMONIZE WITH CRAFTSMAN FURNITURE.

THE KIND OF FABRICS AND NEEDLEWORK THAT HARMONIZE WITH AND COMPLETE THE CRAFTSMAN DECORATIVE SCHEME

WE have traced in this book the development of the Craftsman scheme of building and interior decoration, beginning with the house as a whole and thence working back to an analysis of the different rooms, the wall spaces, struc-

PORTIÈRE OF CRAFTSMAN CANVAS WITH PINE CONE DESIGN IN APPLIQUÉ.

tural features, furnishings and metal work, all of which must be considered separately as essential parts of the complete structure, including the decorative scheme. In doing this we have reversed the process by which we worked out the idea in the first place, for we began ten years ago with the furniture; the metal work followed as a matter of course because it was the next thing needed; then the dressing of leathers to harmonize with the style of the furniture and the wood of which it was made. Then came the finding of suit-

able fabrics and the kind of decoration most in keeping with them, and from all these parts was naturally developed the idea of the Craftsman house as a whole.

At first it was very difficult to find just the right kind of fabric to harmonize with the Craftsman furniture and metal work. It was not so much a question of color, although of course a great deal of the effect depended upon perfect color harmony, as it was a question of the texture and character of the fabric. Silks, plushes and tapestries, in fact delicate and perishable fabrics of all kinds, were utterly out of keeping with Craftsman furniture. What we needed were fabrics that possessed sturdiness and durability; that were made of materials that possessed a certain rugged and straightforward character of fiber, weave and texture,—such a character as

PORTIÈRE OF CRAFTSMAN CANVAS WITH CHECKERBERRY DESIGN IN APPLIQUÉ.

SASH CURTAIN OF TEA-COLORED NET DARNED IN AN OPEN PATTERN WITH SILVER-WHITE FLOSS.

SASH CURTAIN OF CASEMENT LINEN WITH FRETWORK DESIGN IN SOLID DARNED WORK.

would bring them into the same class as the sturdy oak and wrought iron and copper of the other furnishings. Yet they could not be coarse or crude, for that would have taken them as far away from the quality of the furniture on the one side, as plushes and brocades were on the other.

For upholstering the furniture itself we had found leather more satisfying than anything else, especially as by constant experimenting we had succeeded in developing a method of dressing that preserved all the leathery quality in much the same way that we were able to preserve the woody quality of the oak, so that the leather maintained its own sturdy individuality, at the same time possessing a softness and flexibility and a sub-

tlety of coloring that proved wonderfully attractive. This was especially the case with sheepskin, which we finished in all the subtle shades of brown, biscuit, yellow, gray, green, and fawn, but always with the leathery quality predominant under the light surface tone. These leathers accorded so well with the plain oak furniture and metal work that for a time they became almost too popular, for they were used by many people for table covers, portiéres and the like, in rooms where rugged effects were considered desirable. In fact, the fad ran to such lengths that it fortunately wore itself out and leather was allowed to return to its proper uses.

This was made easier by the discovery of certain fabrics that harmonize as completely as leather with the general Craftsman scheme. These are mostly woven of flax left in the natural color or given some one of the nature hues. There are also certain roughly-woven, dull-finished silks that fit into the picture as

SCARF OF HAND-WOVEN LINEN WITH PINE CONE DESIGN IN DARNED WORK.

SASH CURTAIN OF CASEMENT LINEN WITH ANOTHER FORM OF PINE CONE DESIGN DONE IN DARNED WORK.

TABLE SCARF OF UNBLEACHED HAND-WOVEN LINEN WITH DRAGONFLY DESIGN DARNED IN PERSIAN COLORS.

TABLE SCARF WITH GINKGO DESIGN IN APPLIQUÉ OF DEEP LEAF GREEN UPON HOMESPUN LINEN.

well as linen, and for window curtains we use nets and crepes of the same general character. A material that we use more than almost any other for portiéres, pillows, chair cushions,—indeed in all places were stout wearing quality and a certain pleasant unobtrusiveness are required—is a canvas woven of loosely twisted threads of jute and flax and dyed in the piece,—a method which gives an unevenness in color that amounts almost to a two-toned effect because of the way in which the different threads take the dye. This unevenness is increased by the roughness of the texture, which is not unlike that of a firmly woven burlap. The colors of the canvas are delightful. For example, there are three tones of wood brown,—one almost exactly the color of old weather-beaten oak; another that shows a sunny yellowish tone; and a third that comes close to a dark russet. The greens are the foliage hues,—one dark and brownish like rusty pine needles, another a deep leaf-green; the third an intense green like damp grass in the shade; and a fourth a very gray-green with a bluish tinge like the eucalyptus leaf.

Our usual method of decorating this canvas is the application of some bold and simple design in which the solid parts are of linen appliqué in some contrasting shade and the connecting lines are done in heavy outline stitch or couching with linen floss. This sim-

TABLE SCARF OF HOMESPUN LINEN WITH PINE CONE DESIGN IN APPLIQUÉ.

PILLOW COVERED WITH CRAFTSMAN CANVAS AND ORNAMENTED WITH PINE CONE DESIGN IN APPLIQUÉ.

TABLE SCARF FOR A BEDROOM, WITH POPPY DESIGN IN DARNED WORK.

plicity is characteristic of all the Craftsman needlework, which is bold and plain to a degree. We use appliqué in a great many forms, especially for large pieces such as portières, couch covers, pillows and the larger table covers. For scarfs, window curtains and table furnishings of all kinds we are apt to use the simple darning stitch, as this gives a delightful sparkle to any mass of color. For the rest we use the satin stitch very occasionally when a snap of solid color is needed for accenting now and then a bit of plain hem-stitching or drawn work. It is the kind of needlework that any woman can do and, given the power of discrimination and

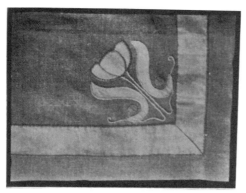

POPPY DESIGN CARRIED OUT IN APPLIQUÉ TO ORNAMENT THE CORNER OF A COUCH COVER.

taste in the selection of materials, designs and color combinations, there is no reason why any woman should not, with comparatively little time and labor, make her home interesting with beautiful and characteristic needlework that is as far removed from the "fancy work" which too often takes the place of it, as any genuine and useful thing is removed from things that are unnecessary.

For scarfs, table squares, luncheon and dinner sets and the like, we find that the most suitable fabrics in connection with the Craftsman furnishings are the linens, mostly in the natural colors and the rougher weaves.

SAME POPPY DESIGN AS APPLIED TO A BEDSPREAD OF HOMESPUN LINEN.

We use hand-woven and homespun linens in many weights and weaves, and a beautiful fabric called Flemish linen, which has a matt finish and is very soft and pliable to the touch. Some of these come in the cream or ivory shades and all of them in the tones of cream gray and warm pale brown natural to the unbleached linen. We find, as a rule, that the finer and more delicate white linens do not belong in a Craftsman room any more than silks, plushes and tapestries in delicate colorings belong with the Craftsman furniture. The whole scheme demands a more robust sort of beauty,—something that primarily exists from use and that fulfils every requirement. The charm that it possesses arises from the completeness with which it answers all these demands and the honesty which allows its natural quality to show.

CABINET WORK FOR HOME WORKERS AND STUDENTS WHO WISH TO LEARN THE FUNDAMENTAL PRINCIPLES OF CONSTRUCTION

IN the brief sketch we have already given of furniture making in this country we made the statement that one of the chief elements of interest in Craftsman furniture is the fact that its construction is so simple and direct and so clearly revealed that any one possessing even a rudimentary knowledge of tools and of drawing and some natural skill of hand could easily make for himself many pieces of furniture in this style. Believing this thoroughly, and also realizing fully the interest that cabinetwork holds for most people and the means it affords of developing the constructive and creative faculties, we have given in THE CRAFTSMAN a number of designs solely for the benefit of home workers. For a year or two we published, in connection with these designs, full working drawings and also mill bills for the necessary lumber; but we were forced to abandon that on account of lack of space and to give only the drawings showing the finished pieces, for which the working drawings and mill bills were easily obtainable upon application.

We illustrate here a number of these designs, most of which are for pieces that are fairly easy to make and that have a definite use as household furnishings. While the designs of course show the exact models of the pieces they represent, we intend them to have also a suggestive value and to stimulate thought and experiment along the lines of designing and making plain substantial furniture. It has been proven beyond question that the most powerful stimulus to well-defined constructive thought is found in the direction of the mind to some form of creative work. Therefore if a man or a boy has any aptitude along these lines, it is a foregone conclusion that he will not have

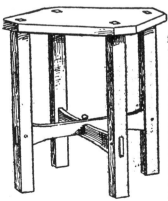

FIGURE ONE.—SQUARE TABOURET.

made many pieces after given models before he begins to think for himself and to make or modify designs to meet his own demands and to afford an opportunity for working out his own problems. Furthermore, as his experience grows, he will naturally discover new ways of doing things that may be better for him to follow than any of the stereotyped rules. We approve thoroughly of the freedom of spirit that leads to such experimenting, for, although we originated the Craftsman furni-

FIGURE TWO.—A ROUND TABOURET.

ture, it is just such interest and work on the part of other people that will ultimately develop it into a national style. One warning, however, we would like to give to all amateur workers: that is, that one's own whims must no more be followed than the whims of other people. We will find plenty of interest and occupation in making things that are actually needed and plenty of exercise for all our creative power in designing them to fulfil as adequately as possible the purpose for which they are intended. So long as this is done there is no danger of the work degenerating into a fad; instead, it is likely not only to give much pleasure and profit to individuals, but to grow until the whole nation once more reaps the benefit that comes from the intelligent exercise of the creative powers in some interesting form of handicraft.

Every one knows the relief to brain workers and to professional men that is found in this kind of work. It not only affords a wholesome change of occupation but brings into play a different set of faculties and so proves both restful and stimulating. A professional or business man who can find relief from his regular work in some such pursuit,

CABINET WORK FOR HOME WORKERS

FIGURE THREE.—HALL BENCH WITH CHEST.

peals to him instead of being taught sound principles of design and construction and so guided by a competent worker that all his own work is based upon these principles and is thoroughly done. If the work is merely regarded as play, the theoretical attitude toward the expression of individuality is all right; but if it is regarded as a preparation for the serious business of later life, the result shows that it unfits the student for real work in just such measure as he shows an aptitude for play work.

The introduction of the Craftsman style has practically revolutionized manual training in our public schools, because it has placed at the disposal of the teachers designs of such simplicity and clearness of construction that the work of teaching has been made much easier and the field of manual training has been greatly broadened. Before the introduction of Craftsman furniture, manual training in the schools rested chiefly upon sloyd, which was confined to the making of small articles entirely for the sake of the mental development afforded by the intelligent use of the hands. Now, however, the students of manual training are learning to

which he takes up as a recreation, does better work in his own vocation because he is a healthier and better balanced man and his interest in his home grows more vivid and personal with every article of furniture that he makes with his own hands and according to his own ideas.

As for the means of education afforded by this kind of work, we have no better proof than is shown by the widespread belief in the efficacy of manual training in our public schools, although to a practical craftsman there would seem to be plenty of room for improvement, both as to methods of teaching and the quality of workmanship that is required from the students. Where manual training is taken up purely on account of the mental development it affords, there is a tendency to make it entirely academic. The teachers for the most part rely almost wholly upon theory and have very little practical knowledge of the thing they teach. The result is that a boy is encouraged to "express his own individuality" in designing and making the thing that ap-

FIGURE FOUR.—CHILD'S OPEN BOOKCASE.

FIGURE FIVE.—CHESS OR CHECKER TABLE.

make furniture after such models as we show here and the very necessary element of usefulness is added to the things they make. The only difficulty is that the craft itself is not well enough understood by the teachers to be imparted to the students in such a way that they derive any permanent benefit from it. The teaching is, as we have said, largely theoretical and the object of the whole training is mental development along general lines rather than the moral development that comes from learning to do useful work thoroughly and well. As cabinet-work is handled in the manual training departments of the schools, it is distinctly a side issue, and exhibitions of the work to which public attention is frequently invited show ambitious pieces of furniture that are wrongly proportioned, badly put together and finished in a slovenly way, thus producing exactly the opposite effect upon the pupil from what is intended. If the State or municipal authorities would see to it that manual training in the form of wood-working of all kinds, and especially the making of furniture, were placed under the charge of thoroughly skilled craftsmen who understood and were able to teach all the principles of construction, the moral and educational effect of such work would be almost incalculable.

In order to make the training of any real value, it is absolutely necessary that the student begin simultaneously with mechanical drawing and the application of its principles

FIGURE SEVEN.—PORTABLE CABINET FOR WRITING TABLE.

to his work as he goes along. If he began with simple models to which could be applied the elementary lessons in mechanical drawing, the laying out of plans, the reading of detail drawings and the like, and would also afford a chance to demonstrate lessons in the use of the square, the level, the saw and the plane;—a good foundation would be laid not only for the understanding of right principles of construction but for the accurate use of tools. A boy trained in this way would be able in future years to put his knowledge to almost any use that was needed. Instead of this the students endeavor to make something that is interesting and that shows well at home or in an exhibition. In fact, the situation now is very much as it would be if a student of music were to take two or three lessons in the rudiments and then endeavor to play a more or less elaborate composition. There is no question as to the benefit that boys, and girls too, derive from being taught to work with their hands; but it is better not to teach them at all than to give them the wrong teaching. No one expects a schoolboy or an amateur worker of any age to make elaborate furniture that would equal similar pieces made by a trained cabinet-maker. But if the student be taught to make small and simple things and to make each one so that it would pass muster anywhere, he learns from the start the fundamental principles of design and proportion and so comes naturally to understand what is meant by thorough workmanship.

There is no objection to any worker, however inexperienced, attempting to express his own

FIGURE SIX.—PIANO BENCH, STRONGLY MADE WITH SOLID ENDS.

CABINET WORK FOR HOME WORKERS

and construction as carefully as he would be grounded in mathematics or classical literature, he might safely be trusted to produce something that would express his own individuality, for then, if ever, he would have developed an individuality that was worth while. And this principle applies as well to amateur workers of all kinds as it does to the students in the public schools, for it is the basis of all work that is worthy to endure.

One great advantage of taking up cabinetmaking at home as well as in the schools, is that it could be made not only a means of amusement or mental development to the individual, but could be expanded into a home or neighborhood handicraft that might be carried on in connection with small farming, upon a basis that would insure a reasonable financial success. Handicrafts, as practiced by individual arts and crafts workers in the studio, do not afford a sufficient living to craft workers as a class, but that is largely because these very principles of sound construction and thorough workmanship are not always observed or even comprehended, so that it is difficult for the individual worker to produce anything that has a definite and permanent commercial value. This kind of furniture, on the contrary, has a very well defined and thoroughly established commercial value, as our own experience has proven; and yet it is so simple in design and construction that it can be made at home or on the farm during the idle months of winter or by a group of

individuality, but the natural thing would be for him to express it in more or less primitive forms of construction that are, so far as they go, correct, instead of attempting something that, when it is finished, is all wrong because the student has not understood what he was about. Unquestionably there are certain principles and rules as to design, proportion and form that are as fundamental in their nature as are the tables of addition, subtraction, division and multiplication, with relation to mathematics, or as the alphabet is as a basis to literature, but they are not yet formulated for general use. The trained worker learns these things by experience and comes to have a sort of sixth sense with regard to their application, but this takes strong direct thinking, keen observation and the power of initiative that is possessed only by the very exceptional and highly skilled workman.

Nevertheless it surely is as easy to begin work in the right way as in the wrong way. It would be better if all our teaching of manual training were based upon some text book carefully compiled by a master workman and kept within certain well defined limits. After the student had thoroughly learned all that lay within these limits and was grounded in the principles of design

172

CABINET WORK FOR HOME WORKERS

FIGURE TEN.—BOOK CABINET.

workers in a village,—in fact under almost any conditions where it would seem advantageous to do such work, especially under the guidance of a competent cabinetmaker.

Whether regarded as one of the forms of a profitable handicraft that might be depended upon as a means of support,—or at least of adding to the income obtained from a small farm,—or whether regarded merely as a means of recreation for a busy man during his leisure hours at home, cabinetmaking is likely to prove a most interesting pursuit. One distinct advantage is that furniture made in this way, if well done, would be better than any that could possibly be made in a factory, because the work would naturally be more carefully done. Also the interest that attaches to the right use of wood could be developed to a much greater degree than is possible where the work is done on a large scale, because judgment and discrimination could be applied to the selection of lumber that is without any special market value according to commercial standards, but that has in it certain flaws and irregularities that make it far more interesting than the costlier lumber necessary for purely commercial work. This one item would be a great advantage as lumber grows scarcer and harder to obtain. Also, the furniture itself would

have much more individual interest because of this very feature, for then it would be possible to select certain pieces of wood for special uses and to develop to the utmost all the natural qualities of color and grain that might prove interesting when rightly used and in the right place. It is by these very methods and under similar conditions that the Japanese have gained such world-wide fame as discriminating users of very simple and inexpensive woods. A Japanese regards a piece of wood as he might a picture and his one idea is to do something with it that will show it to the very best advantage, as well as gain from it the utmost measure of usefulness.

Among the cabinet woods native to this country and easily obtained are white oak, brown ash, rock elm, birch, beech and maple. Chestnut, cypress, pine, redwood and gumwood, while all excellent for interior trim,

FIGURE ELEVEN.—BOOKCASE WITH ADJUSTABLE SHELVES.

FIGURE TWELVE.—SMALL STAND FOR USE IN A BEDROOM.

are not hard enough to give satisfactory results when used for the making of furniture. Of those first mentioned, white oak is unquestionably the best for cabinetmaking and, indeed, it is a wood as well suited to the Craftsman style of furniture as the Spanish mahogany was to the French, English and Colonial furniture of the eighteenth century. Spanish mahogany is very rare now and the modern mahogany, or baywood, is very little harder than whitewood and so cannot be considered particularly desirable as a cabinet wood. The old mahogany was a hard, close-grained, fine-textured wood that lent itself naturally to the slender lines, graceful curves and delicate modeling of the eighteenth century styles. In addition to this the wood itself was so treated as to ripen to the utmost the quality of rich and mellow coloring, which was one of its distinctive characteristics. The boards were kept for months, and some of them for years, in the courtyards of the cabinet shops, where sun and rain could give them the mellowness of age. Then the finished pieces were treated with linseed oil and again put out into the sunshine to oxidize, this process being repeated until the wood gained just the required depth of color and perfection of finish. The slowness of this process and the care and skill required to produce the results that were aimed at makes fine mahogany furniture almost an impossibility today, except to the craftsman who may be able to afford selected pieces of this rare and almost extinct wood, and who has sufficient leisure and love of the work to treat it according to the methods of the old cabinetmakers. Even then it is not suitable for the plain massive furniture that

we show here as models for home workers. The severely plain structural forms that we are considering now demand a wood of strong fiber and markings, rich in color, and possessing a sturdy friendly quality that seems to invite use and wear. The strong straight lines and plain surfaces of the furniture follow and emphasize the grain and growth of the wood, drawing attention to instead of destroying the natural character that belonged to the growing tree. As the use of oak would naturally demand a form that is strong and primitive, the harmony that exists between the form and construction of the furniture and the wood of which it is made is complete and satisfying.

We will then assume that oak is the wood that would naturally be selected by the home cabinetmaker and for large surfaces such as table-tops and large panels, quarter-sawn oak is deemed preferable to plain-sawn, as the first method, which makes the cut parallel with the medullary rays that form the peculiar wavy lines seen in quarter-sawn oak, not only brings out all the natural beauty of the markings, but makes the wood structurally stronger, finer in grain and less liable to check and warp than when it is straight-sawn. Care should then be taken to see that the wood is thoroughly dried, otherwise the best work might easily be ruined by the checking, warping, or splitting of the lumber. Quarter-sawn oak is the hardest of all woods to dry and requires the longest time, so that it would hardly be advisable for the amateur cabinetmaker to attempt to use other than selected kiln-dried wood that is ready for the saw and plane.

FIGURE THIRTEEN.—ROUND TABLE.

CABINET WORK FOR HOME WORKERS

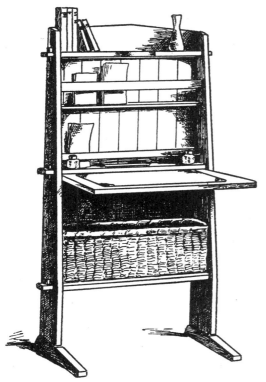

FIGURE FOURTEEN.—WRITING DESK WITH WILLOW WASTE BASKET.

The work of construction must all be done before the wood is given its final finish; but in this connection we will outline briefly the best method of finishing oak, as the sturdy wooden quality of the furniture depends entirely upon the ability of the worker to treat the wood so that there is little evidence of an applied finish. Oak should be ripened as the old mahogany was ripened by oil and sunshine, and this can be done only by a process that, without altering or disguising the nature of the wood, gives it the appearance of having been mellowed by age and use. This process is merely fuming with ammonia, which has a certain affinity with the tannic acid that exists in the wood, and it is the only one known to us that acts upon the glossy hard rays as well as the softer parts of the wood, coloring all together in an even tone so that the figure is marked only by its difference in texture. This result is not so good when stains are used instead of fuming, as staining leaves the soft part of the wood dark and the markings light and prominent.

The fuming is not an especially difficult process, but it requires a good deal of care, for the piece must be put into an air-tight box or closet, on the floor of which has been placed shallow dishes containing aqua ammonia (26 per cent). The length of time required to fume oak to a good color depends largely upon the tightness of the compartment, but as a rule forty-eight hours is enough. When fuming is not practicable, as in the case of a piece too large for any available compartment or one that is built into the room, a fairly good result may be obtained by applying the strong ammonia directly to the wood with a sponge or brush. In either case the wood must be in its natural condition when treated, as any previous application of oil or stain would keep the ammonia from taking effect. After the wood so treated is thoroughly dry from the first application it should be sandpapered carefully with fine sandpaper, then a second coat of ammonia applied, followed by a second careful sandpapering.

Some pieces fume much darker than others, according to the amount of tannin left free to attract the ammonia after the wood has

FIGURE FIFTEEN.—TABLE DESK.

175

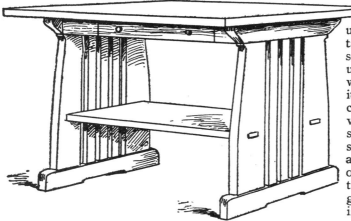

FIGURE SIXTEEN.—LIBRARY TABLE.

ened by the addition of a small quantity of the stain used in touching up. Care must be taken, however, to carry on the color so lightly that it will not grow muddy under the brush of an inexperienced worker. The danger of this makes it often more advisable to apply two coats of lacquer, each containing a very little color. If this is done, sandpaper each coat with very fine sandpaper after it is thoroughly dried and then apply one or more coats of prepared floor wax. These directions, if carefully followed, should give the same effects that characterize the Craftsman furniture.

Sometimes a home cabinetworker does not find it practicable or desirable to fume the oak. In such a case there are a number of good stains on the market that could be used on oak as well as on other woods.

Oak and chestnut alone are susceptible to the action of ammonia fumes, but in other ways the oak, chestnut, ash and elm come into one class as regards treatment, for the reason that they all have a strong, well-defined grain and are so alike in nature that they are affected in much the same way by the same method of finishing. For any one of these woods a water stain should never be used, as it raises the grain to such an extent that in sandpapering to make it smooth again, the color is sanded off with the grain, leaving an unevenly stained and very unpleasant surface. The most satisfactory method we know, especially for workers who have had but little experience, is to use a small amount of color carried on in very thin

been kiln-dried. Where any sap wood has been left on, that part will be found unaffected by the fumes. There is apt also to be a slight difference in tone when the piece is not all made from the same log, because some trees contain more tannic acid than others. To meet these conditions it is necessary to make a "touch-up" to even the color. This is done by mixing a brown aniline dye (that will dissolve in alcohol) with German lacquer, commonly known as "banana liquid." The mixture may be thinned with wood alcohol to the right consistency before using. In touching up the lighter portions of the wood the stain may be smoothly blended with the darker tint of the perfectly fumed parts, by rubbing along the line where they join with a piece of soft dry cheese-cloth, closely following the brush. If the stain should dry too fast and the color is left uneven, dampen the cloth very slightly with alcohol. After fuming, sandpapering and touching up a piece of furniture, apply a coat of lacquer, made of one-third white shellac and two-thirds German lacquer. If the fuming process has resulted in a shade dark enough to be satisfactory, this lacquer may be applied clear; if not, it may be dark-

FIGURE SEVENTEEN.—LARGE LIBRARY TABLE.

176

shellac. If the commercial cut shellac is used it should be reduced with alcohol in the proportion of one part of shellac to three of alcohol. This is because shellac, as it is ordinarily cut for commercial purposes, is mixed in the proportion of four pounds to a gallon of alcohol, so that in order to make it thin enough it is necessary to add sufficient alcohol to obtain a mixture of one pound of shellac to a gallon of alcohol. If the worker does his own cutting he will naturally use the proportion last mentioned,—one pound of shellac to a gallon of alcohol. When the piece is ready for the final finish, apply a coat of thin shellac, adding a little color if necessary; sandpaper carefully and then apply one or more coats of liquid wax. These directions are entirely for the use of home workers. The method we use in the Craftsman Workshops differs in many ways, for we naturally have much greater facilities for obtaining any desired effect than would be possible with the equipment of a home worker.

For lighter pieces of furniture suitable for a bedroom or a woman's sitting room, where dainty effects are desirable, we find maple the most satisfactory, in both color and texture, of our native woods, for the reason that it is

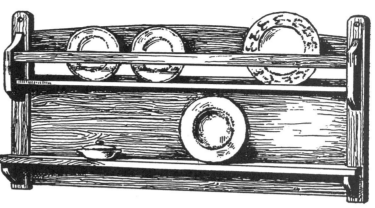

FIGURE NINETEEN.—PLATE RACK TO BE PLACED OVER A SIDEBOARD.

hard enough to be used for all kinds of furniture. Gumwood is equally beautiful, but is not hard enough for chairs. For built-in furniture, however, and for tables, dressers and the like, gumwood is one of the most beautiful woods we have, as it takes on a soft, satin-like texture with variable color effects not unlike those seen in the finest Circassian walnut. We find that the best effect in both maple and gumwood is obtained by treating the wood with a solution of iron-rust made by throwing iron filings or any small pieces of iron into acid vinegar or a weak solution of acetic acid. After forty-eight hours the solution is drained off and diluted with water until the desired color is obtained. The wood is merely brushed over with this solution,—wetting it thoroughly,—and left to dry. This is a process that requires much experimenting with small pieces of wood before attempting to treat the furniture, as the color does not show until the application is completely dry. By this treatment maple is given a beautiful tone of pale silvery gray and the gumwood takes on a soft pale grayish brown, both of which colors harmonize admirably with dull blue, old rose, straw color, or any of the more delicate shades so often used in furnishing a bedroom or a woman's sitting room.

As to the actual construction of the pieces shown here, it is in most cases very simple. By a careful study of the different models it will be noted that the only attempt at decoration lies in the emphasizing of the actual structural features, such as posts, panels, tenons with or without the key, the dovetail joint and the key as

FIGURE EIGHTEEN.—SMALL SIDEBOARD.

CABINET WORK FOR HOME WORKERS

it is used to strengthen and emphasize the joining of two boards. For the rest, the beauty of each piece depends wholly upon the care with which the wood is selected, the proportions and workmanship of the piece, and the attention that is given to the delicate details of construction and to the finish of the wood.

In Figures 1 and 2 we illustrate two of the simplest models we have ever offered for the use of home cabinetworkers. They are two designs for small tabourets and were selected to illustrate the first article on home training in cabinetwork, published in THE CRAFTSMAN in April, 1905. Therefore from the point of view of their precedence in the series, no less than their fitness as models for the beginner, they have been chosen to head the illustrations for this article. In the case of both of them the construction shows for itself. The tenons of the legs are visible through the top of the table, where they are firmly wedged and then planed flush with the top. This not only strengthens the table very considerably, but the difference in the grain of the wood gives the effect of four small square inlays in each table top. Also it is well to note that, in cutting the mortises for the stretchers of the square tabouret, there is half an inch difference in the heights of the two stretchers. A dowel pin three-eighths of an inch in diameter

FIGURE TWENTY-ONE.—SMALL LETTER AND PAPER FILE.

runs all the way through the legs and holds firm the tenons of the stretchers, making it practically impossible for the table to rack apart. These pins are planed off flush with the sides of the legs.

Figures 3 and 6 illustrate companion pieces, the first being a hall bench and the second a piano bench. Both are simple to a degree, yet the proportions are so contrived that the effect of each is individual and decorative. The outward slope of the solid end pieces gives an appearance of great strength that does full justice to the real strength of both benches. The severity of these end pieces is rather lightened by the curved opening at the bottom and by the openings at the top, meant in each case for convenience in moving the bench. These openings, with the slight projections of the tenons at the ends, form the only decoration. In the case of the hall bench, a shallow box takes the place of the curved brace that appears under the seat in the piano bench. This box can be used to hold all sorts of things that ordinarily accumulate in the hall and the hinged seat lifts like a lid over it. The bench can be made in any desired length to fit any wall space without interfering with its construction or proportions.

Figure 4 shows a small open bookcase that is intended for the use of children. All housewives know that one of the greatest difficulties in keeping a tidy nursery often arises because there is no place where children can easily put things away themselves. Closet doors are hard to open and the shelves too high to be of use, while shelves and brackets are usually purposely out of reach and the nursery table is apt to be full. This little bookcase is planned especially to meet just such a nursery problem. There are no doors and the shelves are broad and

FIGURE TWENTY.—COMBINATION TABLE AND ENCYCLOPEDIA BOOKCASE.

low enough to be within the reach of very little children. The shelves are not adjustable but are put in stoutly with tenon and key so that they are never out of place and never need attention.

Figure 5 shows a small table that would prove a convenient piece of furniture in a household where either chess or checkers happens to be a favorite game. The legs are slightly tapering, sloped outward and are made firm with bracket supports so that the usual cross supports below, which would interfere with the comfort of the players sitting at the table, are not needed. The rails under the top are tenoned to the legs. In a case like this, where two or more rails meet with the ends opposite each other, short tenons must be used with two dowel pins in each one to hold it in place. These pins are placed near the edge of the table legs so that they may not interfere with the tenoning of the side rails. It is a good plan to dowel the bracket supports first to the legs and then to the top of the table, in addition to the glue which holds them in place. The small drawer is made in the regular way, being hung from the top instead of running on a center guide as do most of the wider drawers in Craftsman furniture. The checks on the table top may be burned into the wood or a dye or stain may be used for the dark checks.

Figure 7 shows a small portable cabinet that may be placed on the top of any writing table. It is provided with little compartments which are protected by doors with flat key locks and with a shelf and pigeon-holes for papers and books. The piece is perfectly plain except for the slight decorative touch given by the dovetailing at the end, but if the wood is well chosen and the cabinet carefully finished, it will be found an attractive as well as a convenient bit of furniture.

Figure 8 illustrates a child's desk, the making

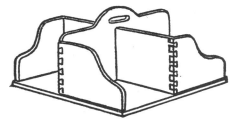

FIGURE TWENTY-TWO.—SMALL REVOLVING BOOK-RACK.

of which would be an especially pleasant piece of work for the home craftsman, because there is no article of miniature furniture which affords the children so much delight as a desk where they can work like grown-up folks and have pads and pencils never to be loaned or lost. This little desk is so simple that the small members of the family might even help to make it and so gain some understanding of the pleasure of making their own belongings. The construction has the same general features that have already been described and the only touch of decoration is the projection of the two back posts above the small upper shelf.

Figure 9 suggests a useful and desirable present for a bride, for it is a cedar-lined chest

FIGURE TWENTY-THREE.—COMBINATION BOOKCASE AND CUPBOARD.

179

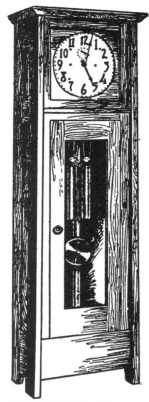

intended for the storing of linen and clothing,—just the same sort of chest as the German maidens use for storing away the linen they weave during their girlhood. In making the chest the legs are first built up, then the front and back fastened in; the ends and bottom are put in at the same time, fitting in grooves. The top is simply made, with two panels divided by a broad stile which affords support for the iron strap-hinge that extends down the side to be fastened with hasp and padlock. The inside of the chest is lined with cedar boards, so desirable for their pleasant aromatic odor and for their moth - preventing properties. This lining should be put in after the chest is made. The iron work can be made by any blacksmith from the drawing, or even made at home if the amateur cabinetworker also possesses a forge.

Figure 10 shows a book cabinet which would be convenient in a workroom, where it might stand near the desk or table of the worker and provide a place for the few books of reference that are in constant use, as well as for papers, drawings and so forth, that might otherwise be mislaid or scattered in confusion about the room. The cabinet is easy to make and is very satisfying in line and proportion. The shelf that covers half the top offers room for a small paper rack or any of the many things that have to be within reach and yet not in the way.

Figure 11 gives a model for a bookcase having two drawers below for papers or magazines and three adjustable shelves that can be moved to any height simply by changing the position of the pegs that support the

shelves. If the books are small, an additional shelf might be put in if required. The frame of the bookcase is left plain, the smooth surface of the sides being broken only by the slightly projecting tenons at the top and bottom. The edges of these tenons are chamfered off and carefully sandpapered so that they have a smooth rounded look. Inside the ends of the bookcase holes about half an inch in diameter are bored about halfway through the thickness of the plank, affording places for the pegs that hold the adjustable shelves.

Figure 12 shows a small table primarily chosen for use in a bedroom, to stand near the bed and hold a lamp or candle and one or two books, but it is convenient in any place where a small stand is needed. The top of the back is to be doweled in place with three half-inch dowel pins and the top itself is fastened to the sides by table fasteners placed under a wide overhang. The drawers should be dovetailed together at the corners and all edges slightly s o f t e n e d by careful sandpapering.

Figure 13. The round table shown here embodies in its construction the same general features as the large square library table shown in Figure 17, only modified to such a degree that the effect is light rather than massive. The braces, top and bottom, are crossed and the four legs are wide and flat, with openings following the lines of the outside. The tenons, which have a bold projection and are fastened with wooden keys, are used as a distinctively decorative feature.

Figure 14 gives a very good idea of a desk which looks hard to make but is not so difficult as might appear at the first glance. The lid can be made first, then the sides and shelves carefully fitted and a quarter-inch iron pin inserted between the sides and the lid so that all

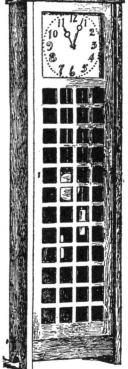

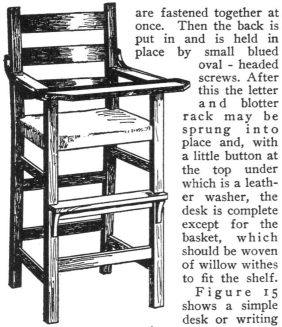

FIGURE TWENTY-SIX.—CHILD'S HIGH CHAIR.

are fastened together at once. Then the back is put in and is held in place by small blued oval - headed screws. After this the letter a n d blotter rack may be sprung into place and, with a little button at the top under which is a leather washer, the desk is complete except for the basket, which should be woven of willow withes to fit the shelf.

Figure 15 shows a simple desk or writing table for the library or living room. The two little upper drawers with the letter file between give a very convenient arrangement for stowing away letters, writing paper, etc. This is a piece which might easily be made crude and heavy, by just a little awkwardness in getting the right proportions and lack of skill in the use of tools; but if carefully made and well finished it possesses a sturdy attractiveness that is very interesting.

Figure 16. This design for a library table should not be attempted until experience in woodwork has taught the worker how to use his tools and materials well. Everything depends upon care both in construction and finishing and especial attention should be given toward maintaining in their integrity all the lines and proportions, as these details have everything to do with making or marring the design. The end pieces, while massive in effect, are relieved from over-heaviness by the use of slats and the shaping of the broad strips on the outside. The top of the table is fastened firmly with table irons so that it is quite solid. Where the shelf tenons come through the end pieces there is a

projection of three-sixteenths of an inch and the edges are chamfered off to give a smooth rounded effect. The tenon itself should be wedged and glued so that it cannot be pulled out. The dovetailing on the drawer may need a little practice before it is successfully executed, but if it is well done it will be a satisfactory evidence of the cleverness of the worker.

Figure 17 shows a large library table that is practically a companion piece to the round table illustrated in Figure 13. In this case, however, the natural massiveness of the construction is emphasized rather than modified, although the severity of the solid ends is softened by the curved lines and open spaces which serve to take away all appearance of clumsiness. The projecting tenons and keys form a suitable structural decoration and add to the strength of the piece. A strong brace just beneath the top keeps the ends firm while the lower shelf acts as another brace.

Figure 18. The lines and proportions of this small sideboard make it an unusually satisfying piece for the home worker to try his skill on because, if it is well made, it is a piece

FIGURE TWENTY-SEVEN.—PORTABLE SCREEN.

FIGURE TWENTY-EIGHT.—RUSTIC BENCH WITH SLAB TOP.

books near at hand. It is meant to hold a complete set of books, with additional space for a dictionary. The plans are so simple that they can be understood and applied by a beginner in cabinetwork and the usefulness of the piece is such as to make it one of the most interesting models we have ever designed for the use of home workers.

Figures 21 and 22 show two most convenient little pieces for a library table. The first is a small letter file with four compartments for note paper, envelopes and letters, making it very useful for the home bookkeeper. The second is a small revolving book rack, made in the form of a swastika, which revolves upon a flat round stand that raises it about an inch from the table. It is meant to hold small books that are needed for constant reference. Both these pieces show to the best advantage the decorative use of the dovetail as a joint. This bit of structural decoration is a favorite with us because we consider the hand-made dovetail to be one of the most interesting structural features used in joinery, as well as the strongest joint. This, of course, applies only to pieces where the strength of the structure depends upon the strength of the corner, for it is purely a corner joint. For example, in the case of this little book-rack the use of the dovetail is almost inevitable, for without it the corners would not only be less perfectly

of furniture that would add much to the beauty of a dining room. The construction, though on a larger scale and in some ways more complicated than in any of the preceding pieces, is no more difficult and no trouble will be found in putting it together. The back is to be screwed into place and is put on last. The top can be doweled on or fastened with table irons. The latter will be safer if there is any doubt as to the thorough seasoning of the wood, as the irons will admit of a slight shrinkage or swelling without cracking the wood. All the edges should be slightly softened with sandpaper just before the finish is applied.

Figure 19. This plate rack is meant to be hung by chains, cords, or heavy picture wire just above the sideboard, although it also serves as a stein rack for a den. The construction speaks for itself and is so simple that nothing need be said about it except that the brackets are fastened with screws from the back. If chains are used to hang it from the rail above, it would be better to have them fairly heavy. Plain round link chains can be bought ready made, together with the hooks, or they can be made to order by any blacksmith.

Figure 20 shows a combination table and encyclopedia bookcase designed especially for the student who wishes to have his reference

FIGURE TWENTY-NINE.—RUSTIC TABLE THAT CAN BE TAKEN APART AT WILL.

FIGURE THIRTY.—RUSTIC SWING SEAT.

joined as regards strength, but the piece would lose its greatest claim to structural interest.

Figure 23 shows a combination bookcase and cupboard with an open shelf in the middle for such books as are most used. The sides have small-paned glass doors and are shelved for books; the central cupboard with the wooden doors is meant to hold papers, magazines and the like.

Figures 24 and 25 show two hall clocks, of the type usually known as the "grandfather's clock." Given a moderate skill in the handling of tools, the home worker can easily make a clock that will prove a quaint and satisfactory

bit of furnishing and will have all the charm of an individual piece of handicraft made for the place it is to fill. Oak is the most appropriate wood for the cases of both these clocks, and the construction is very simple. The face may be made of wood with the figures burned in, or of a twelve-inch plate of brass with figures of copper. If the latter is used, holes should be drilled in the plate to receive the pins which rivet on the figures. These pins are simply bent over after the figures are in place. In both cases the door at the back should have a silk panel in it so that the sound may easily pass through.

Figure 26 shows a child's high-chair designed in the typical Craftsman style. In building this chair put everything together except the arms and when the glue is dry the arm dowels are fitted and the back ones shoved into place. Then by pressure the front will spring into its proper position. All the dowels should be well glued. Care should be used in the joining of the seat rails and it should also be noted that three-eighths of an inch is cut from the bottom of the back post after the chair is put to-

FIGURE THIRTY-ONE.—RUSTIC BED FOR LOG CABIN OR MOUNTAIN CAMP.

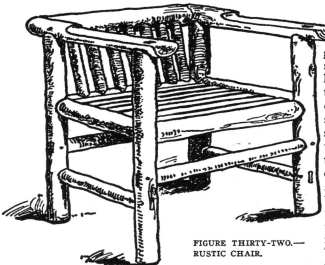

FIGURE THIRTY-TWO.—
RUSTIC CHAIR.

meant for a log cabin or mountain camp. The legs of the bench are made of small logs which are hewn or planed at four angles, leaving the round surface and the wane, so that the piece has in it some of the irregularity of the trunk of the growing tree. The top of the bench is made of a split log planed only at the upper side, the under side being stripped of its bark and left in the natural shape. The horses for the table are made in the same way as the legs of the bench. The table top is in two pieces, the wide thick planks of which it is made being finished as carefully as for any well-made table. These table boards are locked together underneath so that there is no danger of their parting when in use and they can easily be taken apart when it is necessary to move or set aside the table. The great convenience of this table is that it can be taken to pieces and used anywhere, indoors or out.

Figures 30, 31, 32 and 33 show some substantial pieces of rustic furniture designed for country or camp life or for outdoor use. The first is a swinging seat for the veranda or lawn; the second, a bedstead for use in a log cabin or camp; the third is a rustic chair and the fourth a rustic couch for outdoor use. The value of this rustic furniture is not wholly that it is durable and capable of weathering sun and rain alike, but that it makes a special appeal to the amateur carpenter, as its rough exterior hides defects in joining and there is not the special need of well seasoned and carefully prepared lumber that is so essential to the success of the finer pieces.

gether. This makes a little slant back to the seat and gives a comfortable position to the sitter. The back slats of the chair are slightly curved—a thing that can be done by thoroughly wetting or steaming the wood and pressing it into shape and then allowing it to dry. The arms of the adjustable tray are cut from a single piece of wood and the back ends are splined by sawing straight in to a point beyond the curve and inserting in the opening made by the saw a piece of wood cut with the grain and well glued. This device gives strength to a point that otherwise would be very weak.

Figure 27 shows a screen which is very easy to make, yet most decorative, owing to the proportion of the leaves, the curving of the top and the use of keys to hold together the broad V-jointed boards of the lower part. The upper part may be of silk, leather, or any material that is preferred.

Figures 28 and 29 show a rustic bench and table

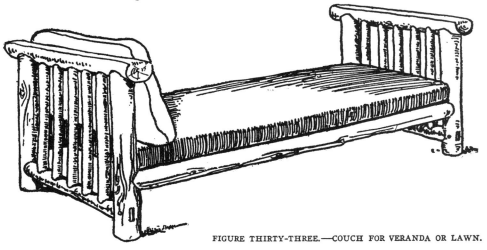

FIGURE THIRTY-THREE.—COUCH FOR VERANDA OR LAWN.

OUR NATIVE WOODS AND THE CRAFTSMAN METHOD OF FINISHING THEM

SO much of the success of the whole Craftsman scheme of building and decoration depends upon the right selection and treatment of the woodwork, which forms such an important part of the structural and also of the decorative scheme, that we have considered it worth while to devote an entire chapter to such information and instruction as we are able to give concerning some of our native woods that we consider most desirable for this purpose. We are taking up only the woods that are native to this country, for the reason that they are nearest at hand and because, when finished by our method, they reveal the beauty of color and grain that forms the basis of the whole Craftsman idea of interior decoration. These vary widely, as each wood possesses strongly marked characteristics as to color, texture and grain; but all the woods we mention here are desirable for interior trim and the use of them is much more in accordance with the Craftsman scheme of decoration than are the elaborate and more or less exotic effects obtained by the use of expensive foreign woods. This does not mean that we claim greater beauty for the native woods, but merely that, when properly treated, they are quite as interesting as any of the more costly woods imported from other countries and have the great advantage of being easily obtainable at moderate cost.

We need not dwell upon the importance of using a generous amount of woodwork to give an effect of permanence, homelikeness and rich warm color in a room. Anyone who has ever entered a house in which the friendly natural wood is used in the form of wainscoting, beams and structural features of all kinds, has only to contrast the impression given by such an interior with that which we receive when we go into the average house, where the plain walls are covered with plaster and paper and the conventional door and window frames are of painted or varnished wood, in order to realize the difference made by giving to the woodwork its full value in the decorative scheme. No care bestowed on decoration, or expense lavished on draperies or furniture, can make up for the absence of wood in the interior of a house. This is a truth that has long been understood and applied in the older countries, especially in England, whose mellow friendly old houses are the delight and despair of Americans; but it is only a few years since we began to apply it to the building and furnishing of our own homes. With us the realization of the possibilities of natural wood when used as a basis for interior decoration first took root in the West, particularly on the Pacific Coast, where the delightful atmosphere of rooms that were wainscoted, ceiled and beamed with California redwood gave rise to a new departure in the finishing and decoration of our homes, and stirred the East to follow suit.

In recommending the generous use of woodwork, however, we would have it clearly understood that we mean the use of wood so finished that its individual qualities of grain, texture and color are preserved so far as possible, and such treatment of wall spaces and structural features that they are not made unduly prominent, but rather sink quietly into the background and become a part of the room itself, forming a friendly unobtrusive setting for the furniture, draperies and ornaments, instead of coming into competition with them. To this end the woodwork should be so finished that its inherent color quality is deepened and mellowed as if by time and its surface made pleasantly smooth without sacrificing the woody quality that comes from frankly revealing its natural texture. When this is done, the little sparkling irregularity of the grain allows a play of light over the surface that seems to give it almost a soft radiance,—a quality that we lose entirely in woodwork that is filled, stained to a solid color, varnished and polished so that the light is reflected from a hard unsympathetic surface.

It is interesting also to note how much the character of a room depends upon the kind of wood we use in it. For example, the impression given by oak is strong, austere and dignified, suggesting stability and permanence such as would naturally belong to a house built to last for generations. It is a robust, manly sort of wood and is most at home in large rooms which are meant for constant use, such as the living room, reception hall, library or dining room. Chestnut, ash and elm,— although each one has an individual quality of color and grain that differentiates it from all the others,—all come into the same class as oak, in that they are strong-fibered, open-textured woods that find their best use in the rooms in which the general life of the household is carried on. The finer-textured woods,

WOODS AND HOW WE FINISH THEM

such as maple, beech, birch and gumwood, are more suitable for the woodwork in smaller and more daintily furnished rooms that are not so roughly used, such as bedrooms or small private sitting rooms. Aside from this general classification, the choice of wood for interior woodwork naturally must depend upon the taste of the home-builder, the requirements of the decorative scheme planned for the house as a whole, and the ease with which a particular kind of wood may be obtained. .

In considering the relative value of our native woods for interior woodwork, we are inclined to give first place to the American white oak, which possesses not only strength of fiber and beauty of color and markings, but great durability, as its sturdiness and the hardness of its texture enables it to withstand almost any amount of wear. In this respect it is far superior to the other woods, such as chestnut, ash and elm, which we have mentioned as being in the same general class of open-textured, strong-fibered woods; although these, under the right treatment, possess a color quality finer than that of oak, in that they show a greater degree of that mellow radiance which counts so much in the atmosphere of a room. This is especially true of chestnut, which is so rich in color that it fairly glows. But in addition to its dignity and durability, there is something about oak that stirs the imagination. Not only is it suggestive of the rich somber time-mellowed rooms of old English houses which have seen generation after generation live and die in them, but it is the wood we are accustomed to associate with nearly all the magnificent carved work of earlier days. In fact, oak has come to stand as a symbol of strength and permanence, and a great part of our affection for it comes from the romance and the rare old associations with which its very name is surrounded.

There are many varieties of oak in this country, but of these the white oak is by far the most desirable, both for cabinetmaking and for interior woodwork. One reason for this is the deep, ripened color it takes on under the process we use for finishing it,—a process which gives the appearance of age and mellowness without in any way altering the character of the wood. We refer to the fuming with ammonia, which we have already described in the preceding chapter. The fact that ammonia fumes will darken new oak was discovered by accident. Some oak boards stored in a stable

in England were found after a time to have taken on a beautiful mellow brown tone and on investigation this change in color was discovered to be due to the ammonia fumes that naturally are present in stables. This ripening, so essential to the beauty of oak woodwork, takes a long time when left to the unaided action of air and sunlight, and the fact that the wood darkened very quickly when it was stored in a stable led to experimenting with the effect of ammonia fumes upon various kinds of oak. The reason for this effect was at first unknown and, to the best of our belief, it was not discovered until the experiments with fuming made in The Craftsman Workshops established the fact that the darkening of the wood was due to the chemical affinity existing between ammonia and tannic acid, of which there is a large percentage present in white oak. This being established, preparations were at once made for using ammonia fumes in a practical way, which we have already described in a preceding chapter. The process mentioned there, however, is practicable only when furniture is to be fumed, as it is quite possible to construct an air-tight compartment sufficiently large to hold one or more pieces of furniture, but when it comes to fuming the woodwork of a whole room it is not so easy. The fuming boxes we use in The Craftsman Workshops are made of tarred canvas stretched tightly over large light wooden frames which are padded heavily around the bottom so that no air can creep in between the box and the floor. The box is drawn to the ceiling by means of a rope and pulley; the furniture is piled directly below and shallow dishes are set around the edges inside the line that marks the limits of the compartment. The box is then lowered almost to the floor; very strong aqua ammonia (26 per cent.) is quickly poured into the dishes and the box dropped at once to the floor. The strength of the ammonia used for this purpose may be appreciated when one remembers that the ordinary ammonia retailed for household use is about 5 per cent.

Of course, for fuming interior woodwork, the air-tight compartment is hardly practicable; but a fairly good substitute for it may be obtained by shutting up the room in which the woodwork is to be fumed, stuffing up all the crevices as if for fumigating with sulphur and then setting around on the floor a liberal number of dishes into which the ammonia is

WOODS AND HOW WE FINISH THEM

poured last of all. It is hardly necessary to say that the person to whom the pouring of the ammonia is entrusted will get out of the room as quickly as possible after the fumes are released.

Another way of treating oak with ammonia is to brush the liquid directly on the wood, but owing to the strength of the fumes this is not a very comfortable process for the worker and it is rather less satisfactory in its results. The ammonia being in the nature of water, it naturally raises the grain of the wood. Therefore, after the application, it should be allowed to dry over night and the grain carefully sandpapered down the next day. As this is apt to leave the color somewhat uneven, the wood should again be brushed over with the ammonia and sandpapered a second time after it is thoroughly dry. This method of getting rid of the grain is by no means undesirable, for the wood has a much more beautiful surface after all the loose grain has been raised and then sandpapered off. Where paint or varnish is used there is no necessity for getting rid of the grain, as it is held down by them. But with our finish, which leaves the wood very nearly in its natural state, it is best to dispose of the loose grain once for all and obtain a natural surface that will remain permanently smooth.

We find the finest white oak in the Middle West and Southwest, especially in Indiana, which has furnished large quantities of the best grade of this valuable wood. Like so many of our natural resources, the once bountiful supply of our white oak has been so depleted by reckless use that it is probable that ten or fifteen years more will see the end of quartered oak, and possibly of the best grades of plain-sawn oak as well. The popularity of quarter-sawn oak,—a very wasteful process of manufacture,—is one of the causes of the rapid depletion of our oak forests. We append a small cut showing the cross-section of a tree trunk marked with the lines made by quarter-sawing. As will be seen, the trunk is first cut into quarters and then each quarter is sawn diagonally from the outside to the center, naturally making the boards narrower and increasing the waste. There is some hope to be derived from the fact that great stretches of oak timberland are now being reforested by the Government, but at best it will be a generation or two before these slow-growing trees are large enough to furnish the best

quality of lumber. There is no question as to the greater durability of quarter-sawn oak for uses which demand hard wear and also where the finer effects are desired, as in furniture, but for interior woodwork plain-sawn oak is not only much less expensive than quartersawn but is quite as desirable in every way. The markings are stronger and more interesting, the difference between the hard and soft parts of the grain is better defined, and the openness of texture gives the wood a mellower color quality than it has when quarter-sawn. The distinguishing characteristic of quartersawn oak is the presence of the glassy rays,—technically called medullary rays,—which bind the perpendicular fibers together and give the oak tree its amazing strength. In quartersawing, the cut is made parallel with these

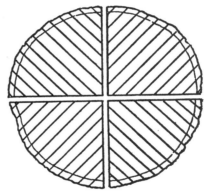

Cross-section of tree-trunk, showing method of quarter-sawing

medullary rays instead of across them, as is done in straight sawing, so that they show prominently, forming the peculiar wavy lines that distinguish quarter-sawn oak. The preservation of the binding properties of these rays gives remarkable structural strength to the wood, which is much less liable to crack, check or warp than when it is plain-sawn. This, of course, makes a difference when it comes to making large panels, table tops, or anything else that shows a large plain surface, and for these uses quarter-sawn oak is preferable merely because it "stands" better. But for the woodwork of a room, we much prefer the plain-sawn oak on account of its friendliness and the delightful play of light and shade that is given by the boldness and color variation of the grain. When quarter-sawn oak is used for large stretches of woodwork, the effect is duller and more austere because the color of the wood is colder and more uniform and it shows a much harder and closer texture.

In the final finishing of oak woodwork, the method that we find most practicable differs somewhat from that described in the directions we have already given for finishing furniture. As the woodwork in a room is not called upon to stand the hard wear that is necessarily given to the furniture, we do not need the shellac, and after the right tone has been obtained by fuming, the wood may be given several coats of prepared floor wax and then rubbed until the surface is satin smooth. If, however, a darker shade of brown is desired, the fumed wood may be given one or more coats of thin shellac, with a little color carried on in each coat, and then finished with wax after the manner described in the directions given for finishing furniture. This method of finishing is one that we have adopted after years of experimenting and it has become so identified with the Craftsman use of oak that it has been very generally taken up by other makers of this style of furniture and by decorators who advocate the Craftsman treatment of interior woodwork.

Next in rank to oak for use in large rooms comes chestnut, which is equally attractive in fiber and markings, has a color quality that is even better, and is plentiful, easily obtained and very reasonable as to cost. While it lacks something of the stateliness and durability of oak, chestnut is even more friendly because of the mellowness and richness of its color, which under very simple treatment takes on a luminous quality that seems to fill the whole room with a soft glow like that of the misty color that is radiated from trees in autumn. Chestnut takes even more kindly than oak to the fuming process, because it contains a greater percentage of tannin and the texture of the wood itself is softer and more open. But unless a deep tone of brown is desired, fuming may be dispensed with, because the wood is so much richer in the elements from which color can be produced that a delightful effect may be obtained merely by applying a light stain of nut brown or soft gray, under which the natural color of the wood appears as an undertone. The staining is very easy to do, but care should be taken to have only a very little color in each coat because the wood takes the stain so readily that a mere trifle of superfluous color will give a thick muddy effect that destroys the clear luminous quality which is

the chief charm. In the case of our Craftsman houses, we find it easier to fume chestnut woodwork than to stain it, and this process is the more to be recommended because chestnut takes the fumes of ammonia very quickly and easily. Also because of this, the ammonia should never be brushed directly on the wood, which is so porous that the moisture is sure to raise the grain to such an extent that the amount of sanding required to smooth it down again destroys the natural surface. One great advantage of chestnut,—aside from its charm of color, texture and markings,—is that it is very easy to work, stays in place readily and is so easy to dry that the chances of getting thoroughly dry lumber are much greater than they would be if oak were used.

Next to chestnut, in our opinion, comes rock elm,—a wood that is fairly abundant, not expensive, and easily obtainable, especially in the East. Rock elm is not affected by the fumes of ammonia and, so far as our experiments go, we have never been able to obtain the right color effect by the use of chemicals. Therefore, in order to get a good color, this wood has to be stained. The colors which are most in harmony with its natural color are brown, green, and gray, particularly in the lighter shades. The distinguishing peculiarity of rock elm is its jagged or feathery grain. Also, the difference in color between the hard and softs parts of the wood is very marked, giving, under the right treatment, a charming variation of tone. If one has the patience to experiment with stains on small pieces of rock elm, some unexpectedly good effects may be obtained. Care must be taken, however, that the stain is light enough to show merely as an over-tone that modifies the natural color of the wood, as the interplay of colors in the grain is hidden by too strong a surface tone. Elm is excellent for interior woodwork where the color effect desired is lighter than that given by either oak or chestnut and also it is hard enough to make pretty good furniture. This last is a decided advantage, especially in a room containing many built-in pieces which naturally form a part of the woodwork. In the earlier days of our experimenting with Craftsman furniture we made a good many pieces of elm and found them, on the whole, very satisfactory.

Brown ash comes into the same class with rock elm, as it is good for furniture as well as interior woodwork. It has a texture and color very similar to elm and should be treated in the same way with a very light stain of either brown, gray or green, all of which blend perfectly with the color quality inherent in the wood. Unfortunately, however, brown ash is no longer plentiful, having been wasted in the same reckless way that we have wasted other excellent woods. Some years ago it was used in immense quantities for making cheap furniture, agricultural implements and the like, and as it was used not only freely but wastefully, the supply is today very nearly exhausted.

In considering all these woods in connection with interior woodwork, it is well to keep in mind that each one of them harmonizes admirably with all the others while retaining, to the full, its own individuality. Therefore, in finishing the rooms on the first floor of a house, it is merely a matter of personal choice as to whether or not the same wood should be used throughout, or each room finished in a different wood. We have often recommended that one wood be used because in a Craftsman house there are practically no divisions or partitions between the rooms, and in this case the effect is so much like that of one large room with many nooks and corners that it would seem the natural thing to use one kind of wood for the interior woodwork throughout. However, if a variation should be desired,— and especially if the separation between the rooms were a little more clearly defined,—the use in different rooms of the different woods we have mentioned would be most interesting, as by this means variety in the woodwork could be obtained without any loss of harmony.

In buildings where it seems desirable to show in the woodwork the bold, strikingly artistic effects such as we associate with Japanese woods, we can heartily recommend cypress, which is plentiful, easily obtained and not expensive. For bungalows, mountain camps, seaside cottages, country clubs and the like, where strong and somewhat unusual effects are sought for, cypress will be found eminently satisfactory, as it is strong and brilliant as to markings and possesses most interesting possibilities in the way of color. Cypress is a soft wood belonging to the pine family and we get most of it from the cypress swamps in the Southern States. It is very like the famous Japanese cypress, which gives such a wonderful charm to many of the Japanese buildings and which is so identified with the Japanese use of woods. Over there they bury

it for a time in order to get the color quality that is most desired,—a soft gray-brown against which the markings stand out strongly and show varying tones. This method, however, did not seem expedient in connection with our own use of the wood and after long experimenting we discovered that we could get much the same effect by treating it with sulphuric acid.

This process is very simple, as it is merely the application of diluted sulphuric acid directly to the surface of the wood. The commercial sulphuric acid should be used rather than the chemically pure, as the first is much cheaper and is quite as good for this purpose. Generally speaking, the acid should be reduced with water in the proportion of one part of acid to five parts of water, but the amount of dilution depends largely upon the temperature in which the work is done. Conditions are best when the thermometer registers seventy-five degrees or more. If it is above that, the sulphuric acid will stand considerably more dilution than it will take if the air is cooler. Of course, in the case of interior woodwork, it is possible to keep the room at exactly the right temperature by means of artificial heat, but when exterior woodwork or shingles are given the sulphuric acid treatment, it is most important to take into consideration the temperature and state of the weather. Exposure to the direct rays of the sun darkens the wood so swiftly that a much weaker solution is required than when the work is done in the shade. In any case, it is best to do a good deal of experimenting upon small pieces of wood before attempting to put the acid on the woodwork itself, as it is only by this means that the exact degree of strength required to produce the best effect can be determined. After the application of the acid the wood should be allowed to dry perfectly before putting on the final finish. For interior woodwork this last finish is given by applying one or two coats of wax; for the exterior, one or two coats of raw linseed oil may be used. If the wood threatens to become too dark under the action of the acid, the burning process can be stopped instantly by an application of either oil or wax, so that the degree of corrosion is largely under the control of the worker. A white hog's-bristle brush should be used for applying the acid, as any other kind of brush would be eaten up within a short time. Also great care should be taken to avoid getting acid on the face, hands, or clothing.

In connection with the subject of cypress for interior woodwork, we desire to say something concerning its desirability for outside use, such as half-timbering and other exterior woodwork. It is one of the most attractive of all our woods for such use because of its color quality and markings and it has the further advantage of "standing" well, without either shrinking or swelling. Naturally the sulphuric acid treatment that we have just described applies to this wood whether it is used indoors or out.

Another use of cypress is found in the rived cypress shingle which give us some of the most interesting effects in exterior wall surfaces. These shingles are the product of one of our few remaining handicrafts, and our sole source of supply depends upon the negroes in the Southern swamps. These negroes are adepts at splitting or riving shingles, and when they get the time or need a little extra money, they split up a few cypress logs into shingles and carry them to a lumber merchant in the nearest town. Consequently, the quantity that is available in the market varies, as no merchant has any great or steady supply of rived shingles and has to accumulate them by degrees and store them, in order to be able to fill any large order. Being hand-rived, these shingles cost about twice as much as the machine-sawn shingles, but they are well worth the extra outlay if one desires a house that is beautiful, individual and durable. The sawn shingle, unless oiled or stained in the beginning, is apt to get a dingy, weather-beaten look under the action of sun and rain and to require renewing early and often. But the rived shingle has exactly the surface of the growing tree from which the bark has been stripped; or, to be more exact, it shows the split surface of a tree trunk from which a bough has been torn, leaving the wood exposed. This surface, while full of irregularities, preserves the smooth natural fiber of the tree, and this takes on a beautiful color quality under the action of the weather, as the color of the wood ripens and shows as an undertone below the smooth silvery sheen of the surface,—an effect which is entirely lost when this natural glint is covered with the "fuzz" left by the saw. These rived shingles are also made of juniper, which is as good in color as cypress and has proven itself even more durable.

All cypress woodwork, whether interior or exterior, takes stain well; and if staining is preferred to the sulphuric acid treatment, very good effects may be gained in this way. We wish, however, to repeat the caution against using too strong a stain, as the effect is always much better if a very little color is carried on in each coat. We cannot too strongly urge the necessity of preliminary experimenting with small pieces of wood in order to gain the best color effects, and we also recommend that in finishing the woodwork of the room itself a very light color be put on at first, to be darkened if a deeper color is found necessary to give the desired effect. The reason for this is that a color which may be considered perfect upon a small piece of wood that is examined closely and held to the light, may prove either too strong or too weak when it is seen on the woodwork as a whole. Much of the effect depends upon the lighting of the room, and therefore it is best to go slowly and "work up" the finish of the woodwork until exactly the right effect is gained. After staining cypress woodwork it should be given either a coat of shellac or wax, or of wax alone, if the amount of wear does not necessitate shellac.

California redwood, when used for interior woodwork, gives an effect as interesting as that obtained by the use of cypress; but redwood does not respond well to the sulphuric acid treatment, which darkens and destroys its beautiful cool pinkish tone. In fact, redwood is best when left in its natural state and rubbed down with wax, as it then keeps in its purity the color quality that naturally belongs to it. Except for this slight finish and protection to the surface, it is a good wood to let alone, as either oil or varnish gives it a hot red look that is disquieting to live with and does not harmonize with any cool tones in the furniture; stains disguise the charm of its natural color and the chemical treatment brings out a purplish tone and gives a darkened and rather muddy effect.

While hard pine is fairly plentiful and lends itself well either to the sulphuric acid treatment or to simple staining, we do not recommend it for interior woodwork, as it costs no less than other woods we have mentioned and is less interesting in color and grain. But if it should be preferred, we would recommend that it be treated with the sulphuric acid, which gives a soft gray tone to the softer parts of

WOODS AND HOW WE FINISH THEM

the wood and a good deal of brilliancy to the markings.

In considering the woods that are most desirable for woodwork in rooms where light colors and dainty furnishings are used, birch comes first on the list, as it is nearest in character to the open-textured woods we have just described. Of the several varieties, red birch is best for interior woodwork. It is easily obtained all over the East, the Middle West and the South and costs considerably less than the other woods we have mentioned. When left in its natural state and treated with sulphuric acid, red birch makes really beautiful interior woodwork, as the acid deepens its natural color and gives it a mellowness that is as fine in its way as the mellowness produced in oak or chestnut by fuming. Some such treatment is absolutely necessary, for if red birch is left in its natural state, its color fades instead of ripening, so that it gets more and more of a washed-out look as time goes on. In using the acid on birch it is necessary to have a stronger solution than is required in the case of cypress; one part of acid to three parts of water should give it about the required strength. One advantage of birch is its hardness, for after the acid treatment it needs only waxing and rubbing to give it the final finish. The good qualities of birch, treated in this way and used for interior woodwork, are very little known, because it is the wood which has been used more than any other to imitate mahogany. The grain of birch is very similar to that of the more expensive wood, and when it has been given a red water stain and finished with shellac and varnish it bears a close resemblance to mahogany finished in the modern way,—which is by no means to be confused with the rare old Spanish mahogany of the eighteenth century.

Another excellent wood for use in a room that should have comparatively fine and delicate woodwork is maple, which can either be left in its natural color or finished in a tone of clear silver gray. As is well known, the natural maple takes on with use and wear a tone of clear pale yellow. This is not considered generally desirable, but if it should be needed to complete some special color scheme, it can be given to new maple by the careful use of aqua fortis, which should be diluted with water and used like sulphuric acid. The same precautions should be observed in using it, as it is a strong corrosive. Maple is generally considered much more beautiful when finished in the gray tone, as this harmonizes admirably with the colors most often used in a daintily furnished room,—such as dull blue, old rose, pale straw color, reseda green and old ivory. It is not at all difficult to obtain this gray finish, for all that is needed is to brush a weak solution of iron rust on the wood. This solution is not made by using oxide of iron,—which is commonly but erroneously supposed to mean the same thing as iron rust,—but is obtained by throwing iron filings, rusty nails or any small pieces of iron into acid vinegar or a weak solution of acetic acid. After a couple of days the solution should be strained off and diluted with water until it is of the strength needed to get the desired color upon the wood. It is absolutely necessary in the case of this treatment to experiment first with small pieces of wood before the solution is applied to the woodwork as a whole, because otherwise it would be impossible to judge as to the strength of solution needed to give the desired effect. The color does not show at all until the application is thoroughly dry. If it is too weak, the wood will not be gray enough, and if it is too strong, it will be dark and muddy looking, sometimes almost black. After the woodwork so treated is perfectly dry and has been carefully sandpapered with very fine sandpaper, it should be given a coat of thin shellac that has been slightly darkened by putting in a few drops of black aniline (the kind that is soluble in alcohol); then it is given the final finish by rubbing with wax. These are the only methods we know that give good results on maple. We have tried the sulphuric acid treatment upon this wood, but have not found it satisfactory.

Beech, which is a little darker than maple and of a similar texture and grain, is equally desirable for the same uses. It may be treated either with iron rust or aqua fortis, following the same directions given in the case of maple. This wood is cheap and abundant and is usually found in the same regions which produce birch and maple. Poplar also does very well for the woodwork in a room that is not subjected to hard wear, as it is a very soft wood and will not stand hard usage. The best finish is simply a brown or green stain thin enough to allow the natural color of the wood to show through it. This natural color has in it a strong suggestion of green, so that it affiliates with the green stain and modifies the brown.

One wood that hitherto has been very little known, but that is coming more and more into prominence for the finer sorts of interior woodwork, is gumwood, which is obtained from the red gum that grows so abundantly in the Southern States and on the Pacific Coast. It is a pity that this beautiful wood should have been so little used that most people are unfamiliar with it, because for woodwork where fine texture, smooth surface and delicate coloring are required, quarter-sawn gumwood stands unsurpassed among our native woods. The best effects are obtained from gumwood by treating it with the iron-rust solution used in the way already described in connection with maple; but much more diluted, as the color of gumwood needs only the slightest possible mellowing and toning to make it perfect. When treated with a very weak iron-rust solution it bears a close resemblance to Circassian walnut, and the surface, which is smooth and lustrous as satin, shows a delightful play of light and shade. Sulphuric acid may be used on gumwood, but should be much more diluted than for any other wood, the proportion of acid being not more than one part to eight parts of water. This treatment gives a pinkish cast to the natural gray-brown tone of the wood, and while this does not harmonize as readily with most colors as does the pure gray-brown, it is very effective with certain decorative schemes.

Other woods that are valuable for interior woodwork, although much less plentiful than those we have named, are black walnut, butternut, quartered sycamore and several other woods that come naturally into the same class. Our American black walnut, although one of the standard woods in Europe, has been in a great measure spoiled for us because of its abuse during what we now speak of as the "black walnut period," which has come to mean over-ornamentation, distorted shapes and general bad taste. We have no forests of black walnut left, but there are still single trees, so that if this wood is especially desired, it may be obtained without much difficulty. The characteristics of butternut are much the same as those of black walnut, but it is rather lighter in color and not so hard.

Many people prefer white enameled woodwork for daintily furnished rooms. When this is used, the best kinds of wood for the purpose are poplar and basswood, preferably poplar. One thing should be remembered in connection with white woodwork, and that is that it should be treated in an entirely different way from the typical Craftsman woodwork, which depends for its effect upon the beauty of color and grain and therefore emphasizes these by means of simple forms, straight lines and plain surfaces. When white enameled woodwork is used, the style of it should be more elaborate, as all the interest that naturally belongs to the wood is hidden, and the only way to obtain the play of light and shade necessary to break up the monotony of the white surface is to use moldings, beadings and similar ornamentation, after what is called the Adam style, which we find in the best of our Colonial houses.

In considering interior woodwork one point should not be forgotten; that is the great interest that may be obtained by the right use of what, from a commercial point of view, is faulty wood. We all know the interest and charm of paneling and other woodwork that displays irregularities in the grain, such as knots, knurls and all sorts of queer twists. One of the best examples is found in the "curly" redwood, which is so greatly sought after in California. While the use of such pieces adds greatly to the beauty of a room, the selection of them requires much taste and judgment and absolutely demands that the personal attention of the owner or decorator be given to the work. It is never safe to trust the selection of faulty wood to the lumber merchant or its placing to the carpenter. The necessity of this care is rather an advantage than otherwise, because it is upon just such touches as these that much of the individuality of a decorative scheme depends.

We have treated fully the selection and coloring of the wood, but one practical detail that should be remembered by all who desire beautiful woodwork is that particular attention should be paid to having all the wood thoroughly kiln-dried. Even more important is the necessity of having the house free from dampness before the woodwork is put in, because no wood, however dry and well seasoned, will stand against the dampness of a newly plastered house. In fact, the effect upon the woodwork in such a case is almost worse than when the wood itself is not thoroughly seasoned, for in the latter case it will merely shrink, while dampness in the house will cause it to swell and bulge. The drying of wood not only needs close attention but the aid of some experienced person, as kiln-dried lumber is very apt to be uneven, and there is need of very careful watching while the wood is in the kiln to insure the even drying of all the boards, or the woodwork will be ruined.

Another thing that is worth watching is the final smoothing of the wood before it is put into place. After it leaves the planing machines in the mill it has to be made still smoother, and so most mills that furnish interior trim have installed sandpapering machines. These are convenient and labor-saving, but give a result that is very undesirable for fine woodwork, as the rotary sanding "fuzzes" the grain and, under the light finish we use, it is apt to be raised and roughened by moisture absorbed from the atmosphere. This does not matter when the woodwork is varnished, because the varnish holds it down, but where the natural surface of the wood is preserved great care should be used in the treatment of the grain. The popularity of Craftsman furniture and interior woodwork has created a demand for a surface that shows the sheen of the knife rather than the fuzz of the sanding machine, and some mills have met this demand by putting in scraping machines. These give better results than the sanding machines, but nothing equals the surface that is obtained by smoothing the wood by hand just before it is put into place. For this we use the hand scraper and a smoothing plane that is kept very sharp, as by this method the fiber is cut clean instead of being "cottoned out" and the sheen that naturally belongs to the wood is unimpaired. Although this means hand work, it is not very expensive because of the inconsiderable quantity of wood that is used in a house. Also the Craftsman method of finishing afterward costs so little that the slight extra care and expense incurred in obaining just the right surface is well worth while.

In connection with the woodwork in a house it is necessary to give some attention to the floors, which come into close relation with the treatment of the walls. The best wood for flooring is quartered oak, which all lumber merchants keep in stock in narrow widths, tongued and grooved. We find, however, that a more interesting floor can be made by using wider boards of uneven width, as this gives an effect of strength and bigness to the room. These wide boards need not be tongued and grooved, but may be put together with butt joints and the boards nailed through the top by using brad-head nails that can be countersunk and the holes puttied up so that they are almost invisible. When very wide boards are used it is best to build the floor in "three ply," like paneling. Plain-sawn oak is also good for flooring, but it is more likely to warp and sliver than quartered oak and it does not lie so flat. An oak floor, whether plain or quarter-sawn, must always be filled with a silex wood filler so that its surface is made smooth and non-absorbent. The color should be made the same as that of the woodwork, or a little darker; and after the stain is applied, the floor should be given one coat of shellac and then waxed. In rooms where the color schemes permit a slightly reddish tone in the floor, we would suggest that either birch or beech be used for flooring, as these may be finished by the sulphuric acid process,—a method which is better than stain because it darkens the wood itself and therefore does not wear off with use. If a gray floor should be desired, we would suggest maple treated with the iron-rust solution. In either case a coat of thin shellac should be applied after the chemical has been thoroughly dried,—say twenty-four hours after the first application,— and then waxed in the regular way. For ordinary floors a good wood to use is comb-grained pine, which receives its name from the method of sawing that leaves the grain in straight lines, not unlike the teeth of a comb. This does not warp or sliver and is very durable; it may be treated with stain and then given the regular finish of shellac and wax.

THE CRAFTSMAN IDEA OF THE KIND OF HOME ENVIRONMENT THAT WOULD RESULT FROM MORE NATURAL STANDARDS OF LIFE AND WORK

IN this book we have endeavored to set forth as fully as possible the several parts which, taken together, go to make up the Craftsman idea of the kind of home environment that tends to result in wholesome living. We have shown the gradual growth of this idea, from the making of the first pieces of Craftsman furniture to the completed house which has in it all the elements of a permanently satisfying home. But we have left until the last the question of the right setting for such a home and the conditions under which the life that is lived in it could form the foundation for the fullest individual and social development.

There is no question now as to the reality of the world-wide movement in the direction of better things. We see everywhere efforts to reform social, political and industrial conditions; the desire to bring about better opportunities for all and to find some way of adjusting economic conditions so that the heart-breaking inequalities of our modern civilized life shall in some measure be done away with. But while we take the greatest interest in all efforts toward reform in any direction, we remain firm in the conviction that the root of all reform lies in the individual and that the life of the individual is shaped mainly by home surroundings and influences and by the kind of education that goes to make real men and women instead of grist for the commercial mill.

That the influence of the home is of the first importance in the shaping of character is a fact too well understood and too generally admitted to be offered here as a new idea. One need only turn to the pages of history to find abundant proof of the unerring action of Nature's law, for without exception the people whose lives are lived simply and wholesomely, in the open, and who have in a high degree the sense of the sacredness of the home, are the people who have made the greatest strides in the development of the race. When luxury enters in and a thousand artificial requirements come to be regarded as real needs, the nation is on the brink of degeneration. So often has the story repeated itself that he who runs may read its deep significance. In our own country, to which has fallen the heritage of all the older civilizations, the course has been swift, for we are yet close to the memory of the primitive pioneer days when the nation was building, and we have still the crudity as well as the vigor of youth. But so rapid and easy has been our development and so great our prosperity that even now we are in some respects very nearly in the same state as the older peoples who have passed the zenith of their power and are beginning to decline. In our own case, however, the saving grace lies in the fact that our taste for luxury and artificiality is not as yet deeply ingrained. We are intensely commercial, fond of all the good things of life, proud of our ability to "get there," and we yield the palm to none in the matter of owning anything that money can buy. But, fortunately, our pioneer days are not ended even now and we still have a goodly number of men and women who are helping to develop the country and make history merely by living simple natural lives close to the soil and full of the interest and pleasure which come from kinship with Nature and the kind of work that calls forth all their resources in the way of self-reliance and the power of initiative. Even in the rush and hurry of life in our busy cities we remember well the quality given to the growing nation by such men and women a generation or two ago and, in spite of the chaotic conditions brought about by our passion for money-getting, extravagance and show, we have still reason to believe that the dominant characteristics of the pioneer yet shape what are the salient qualities in American life.

To preserve these characteristics and to bring back to individual life and work the vigorous constructive spirit which during the last half-century has spent its activities in commercial and industrial expansion, is, in a nut-shell, the Craftsman idea. We need to straighten out our standards and to get rid of a lot of rubbish that we have accumulated along with our wealth and commercial supremacy. It is not that we are too energetic, but that in many ways we have wasted and misused our energy precisely as we have wasted and misused so many of our wonderful natural resources. All we really need is a change in our point of view toward life and a keener perception regarding the things that count and the things which merely burden us. This being the case, it would seem obvious that the place to begin a readjustment is in the home, for it is only natural that the relief from friction which would follow the ordering of our lives along more simple and reasonable lines would not only assure greater comfort, and therefore greater efficiency, to the workers of the nation, but would give the children a chance to grow up under conditions which would be conducive to a higher degree of mental, moral and physical efficiency.

THEREFORE we regard it as at least a step in the direction of bringing about better conditions when we try to plan and build houses which will simplify the work of home life and add to its wholesome joy and comfort. We have already made it plain to our readers that we do not believe in large houses with many rooms elaborately decorated and furnished, for the reason that these seem so essentially an outcome of the artificial conditions that lay such harassing burdens upon modern life and form such a serious menace to our ethical standards. Breeding as it does the spirit of extravagance and of discontent which in the end destroys all the sweetness of home life, the desire for luxury and show not only burdens beyond his strength the man who is ambitious to provide for his wife and children surroundings which are as good as the best, but taxes to the utmost the woman who is trying to keep up the appearances which she believes should belong to her station in life. Worst of all, it starts the children with standards which, in nine cases out of ten, utterly preclude the possibility of their beginning life on their own account in a simple and sensible way. Boys who are brought up in such homes are taught, by the silent influence of their early surroundings, to take it for granted that they must not marry until they are able to keep up an establishment of equal pretensions, and girls also take it as a matter of course that marriage must mean something quite as luxurious as the home of their childhood or it is not a paying investment for their youth and beauty. Everyone who thinks at all deplores the kind of life that marks a man's face with the haggard lines of anxiety and makes him sharp and often unscrupulous in business, with no ambition beyond large profits and a rapid rise in the business world. Also we all realize regretfully the extrava-

THE CRAFTSMAN IDEA

gance and uselessness of many of our women and admit that one of the gravest evils of our times is the light touch-and-go attitude toward marriage, which breaks up so many homes and makes the divorce courts in America a by-word to the world. But when we think into it a little more deeply, we have to acknowledge that such conditions are the logical outcome of our standards of living and that these standards are always shaped in the home.

That is why we have from the first planned houses that are based on the big fundamental principles of honesty, simplicity and usefulness,—the kind of houses that children will rejoice all their lives to remember as "home," and that give a sense of peace and comfort to the tired men who go back to them when the day's work is done. Because we believe that the healthiest and happiest life is that which maintains the closest relationship with out-of-doors, we have planned our houses with outdoor living rooms, dining rooms and sleeping rooms, and many windows to let in plenty of air and sunlight. The most cursory examination of the floor plans given in this book will show that we have put into practical effect our conviction that a house, whatever its dimensions, should have plenty of free space unencumbered by unnecessary partitions or over-much furniture. Therefore we have made the general living rooms as large as possible and not too much separated one from the other. It seems to us much more friendly, homelike and comfortable to have one big living room into which one steps directly from the entrance door,—or from a small vestibule if the climate demands such a protection,—and to have this living room the place where all the business and pleasure of the common family life may be carried on. And we like it to have pleasant nooks and corners which give a comfortable sense of semi-privacy and yet are not in any way shut off from the larger life of the room. Such an arrangement has always seemed to us symbolic of the ideal conditions of social life. The big hospitable fireplace is almost a necessity, for the hearth-stone is always the center of true home life, and the very spirit of home seems to be lacking when a register or radiator tries ineffectually to take the place of a glowing grate or a crackling leaping fire of logs.

Then too we believe that the staircase, instead of being hidden away in a small hall or treated as a necessary evil, should be made one of the most beautiful and prominent features of the room, because it forms a link between the social part of the house and the upper regions which belong to the inner and individual part of the family life. Equally symbolic is our purpose in making the dining room either almost or wholly a part of the living room, for to us it is a constant expression of the fine spirit of hospitality to have the dining room, in a way, open to all comers. Furthermore, such an arrangement is a strong and subtle influence in the direction of simpler living because entertainment under such conditions naturally grows less elaborate and more friendly,—less alien to the regular life of the family and less a matter of social formality.

Take a house planned in this way, with a big living room made comfortable and homelike and beautiful with its great fireplace, open staircase, casement windows, built-in seats, cupboards, bookcases, sideboard and perhaps French doors opening out upon a porch which links the house with the garden; fill this room with soft rich restful color, based upon the mellow radiance of the wood tones and sparkling into the jeweled high lights given forth by copper, brass,

196

or embroideries; then contrast it in your own mind with a house which is cut up into vestibule, hall, reception room, parlor, library, dining room and den,—each one a separate room, each one overcrowded with furniture, pictures and bric-a-brac,—and judge for yourself whether or not home surroundings have any power to influence the family life and the development of character. If you will examine carefully the houses shown in this book, you will see that they all form varying expressions of the central idea we have just explained, although each one is modified to suit the individual taste and requirements of the owner. This is as it should be, for a house expresses character quite as vividly as does dress and the more intimate personal belongings, and no man or woman can step into a dwelling ready made and decorated according to some other person's tastes and preferences without feeling a sense of strangeness that must be overcome before the house can be called a real home.

It will also be noticed in examining the plans of the Craftsman houses that we have paid particular attention to the convenient arrangement of the kitchen. In these days of difficulties with servants and of inadequate, inexperienced help, more and more women are, perforce, learning to depend upon themselves to keep the household machinery running smoothly. It is good that this should be so, for woman is above all things the home maker and our grandmothers were not far wrong when they taught their daughters that a woman who could not keep house, and do it well, was not making of her life the success that could reasonably be expected of her, nor was she doing her whole duty by her family. The idea that housekeeping means drudgery is partly due to our fussy, artificial, overcrowded way of living and partly to our elaborate houses and to inconvenient arrangements. We believe in having the kitchen small, so that extra steps may be avoided, and fitted with every kind of convenience and comfort; with plenty of shelves and cupboards, open plumbing, the hooded range which carries off all odors of cooking, the refrigerator which can be filled from the outside,—in fact, everything that tends to save time, strength and worry. In these days the cook is an uncertain quantity always and maids come and go like the seasons, so the wise woman keeps herself fully equipped to take up the work of her own house at a moment's notice, by being in such close touch with it all the time that she never lays down the reins of personal government. The Craftsman house is built for this kind of a woman and we claim that it is in itself an incentive to the daughters of the house to take a genuine and pleasurable interest in household work and affairs, so that they in their turn will be fairly equipped as home makers when the time comes for them to take up the more serious duties of life.

WE HAVE set forth the principles that rule the planning of the Craftsman house and have hinted at the kind of life that would naturally result from such an environment. But now comes one of the most important elements of the whole question,—the surroundings of the home. We need hardly say that a house of the kind we have described belongs either in the open country or in a small village or town, where the dwellings do not elbow or crowd one another any more than the people do. We have planned houses for country living because we firmly believe that the country is the only place to live in.

THE CRAFTSMAN IDEA

The city is all very well for business, for amusement and some formal entertainment,—in fact for anything and everything that, by its nature, must be carried on outside of the home. But the home itself should be in some place where there is peace and quiet, plenty of room and the chance to establish a sense of intimate relationship with the hills and valleys, trees and brooks and all the things which tend to lessen the strain and worry of modern life by reminding us that after all we are one with Nature.

Also it is a fact that the type of mind which appreciates the value of having the right kind of a home, and recognizes the right of growing children to the most natural and wholesome surroundings, is almost sure to feel the need of life in the open, where all the conditions of daily life may so easily be made sane and constructive instead of artificial and disintegrating. People who think enough about the influence of environment to put interest and care into the planning of a dwelling which shall express all that the word "home" means to them, are usually the people who like to have a personal acquaintance with every animal, tree and flower on the place. They appreciate the interest of planting things and seeing them grow, and enjoy to the fullest the exhilarating anxiety about crops that comes only to the man who planted them and means to use them to the best advantage. Then again, such people feel that half the zest of life would be gone if they were to miss the fulness of joy that each returning spring brings to those who watch eagerly for the new green of the grass and the blossoming of the trees. They feel that no summer resort can offer pleasures equal to that which they find in watching the full flowering of the year; in seeing how their own agricultural experiments turn out, and in triumphing over each success and each addition to the beauty of the place that is their own. Few of these people, too, would care to miss the sense of peace and fulfilment in autumn days, when the waning beauty of the year comes into such close kinship with the mellow ripeness of a well-spent life that has borne full fruit. And what child is there in the world who would spend the winter in the city when there are ice-covered brooks to skate on, the comfort of jolly evenings by the fire and the never-ending wonder of the snow? And all the year round there are the dumb creatures for whom we have no room or time in the city,—the younger brothers of humanity who submit so humbly to man's dominion and look so placidly to him for protection and sustenance.

THANK heaven, though, we are not so far away from our natural environment that it needs much to take us back to it. We have many evidences of the turning of the tide of home life from the city toward the country. Even workers in the city are coming more and more to realize that it is quite possible to maintain their place in the business world and yet give their children a chance to grow up in the country. Also the economic advantage of building a permanent home instead of paying rent year after year is gaining an ever-increasing recognition, so that in a few years the American people may cease to deserve the reproach of being a nation of flat-dwellers and sojourners in family hotels. The instinct for home and for some tie that connects us with the land is stronger than any passing fashion, and although we have in our national life phases of artificiality that are demoralizing they affect only a small percentage of the whole people, and when their day is over they will be forgotten as completely as if they had never existed. Psychologists talk learnedly of "Americanitis" as being almost a national malady, so widespread is our restlessness and feverish activity; but it is safe to predict that, with the growing taste for wholesome country life, it will not be more than a generation or two before our far-famed nervous tension is referred to with wonder as an evidence of past ignorance concerning the most important things of life.

And when we have turned once more to natural living instead of setting up our puny affairs and feverish ambitions to oppose the quiet, irresistible course of Nature's law, we will not need to turn hungrily to books for stories of a bygone Golden Age, nor will we need to deplore the vanishing of art and beauty from our lives, for when the day comes that we have sufficient courage and perception to throw aside the innumerable petty superfluities that hamper us now at every turn and the honesty to realize what Nature holds for all who turn to her with a reverent spirit and an open mind, we will find that art is once more a part of our daily life and that the impulse to do beautiful and vital creative work is as natural as the impulse to breathe.

Therefore it is not idle theorizing to prophesy that, when healthful and natural conditions are restored to our lives, handicrafts will once more become a part of them, because two powerful influences will be working in this direction as they have worked ever since the earliest dawn of civilization. One is the imperative need for self-expression in some form of creative work that always comes when the conditions of life are such as to allow full development and joyous vigor of body and mind. The other is that which closer relationship with Nature seems to bring; a craving for greater intimacy with the things we own and use. Machine-made standards fall away of themselves as we get away from artificial conditions. It is as if wholesome living brought with it not only quickened perceptions but also a sense of personal affection for all the familiar surroundings of our daily life. It is from such feeling that we get the treasured heirlooms which are handed down from generation to generation because of their associations and what they represent.

Naturally the primitive conditions of pioneer life in any nation include handicrafts as a matter of course, from the simple fact that people had to make for themselves what they needed or go without. We realize that in this age of invention and of labor-saving machinery it is neither possible nor desirable to return to such conditions, but we believe that it is quite possible for a higher form of handicrafts to exist under the most advanced modern conditions and that achievements as great as those of the old craftsmen who made famous the Mediæval guilds are by no means out of the reach of modern workers when they once realize the possibilities that lie in this direction. Our theory is that modern improvements and conveniences afford a most welcome and necessary relief from the routine drudgery of household and farm work by disposing quickly and easily of what might much better be done by machinery than by hand, and that therefore there should be sufficient leisure left for the enjoyment of life and for the doing of work that is really worth while, which are among the things most essential to all-round mental and moral development. Almost the greatest drawback to farm life as it is today is the lack of interest and of mental alertness.

Especially is this the case during the winter months, when work on the farm is slack and much time is left to be spent in idleness or in some trifling occupation. Consider what the effect would be if it were made possible at such times to take up some form of creative work that would not only bring into play every atom of interest and ability, but would also serve a practical purpose by adding considerably to the family income!

WE HAVE given a great deal of consideration to the practical side of such a combination of handicrafts and farming, and we realize of course that the great difficulty in the way of making such a thing possible by making it profitable is the question of obtaining a steady market for the products of such crafts as might be practiced in connection with country life. It is often urged as an argument against handicrafts that hand-made goods could not possibly compete with factory-made goods, and that it would be absurd for people to waste time in making things for which there would be no sale. This does not seem to us to be the case, for the reason that there is no competition between the products of handicrafts and factory-made goods, because they are not measured by the same standard of value nor do they appeal to the same class of consumer. Hand-made articles have a certain intrinsic value of their own that sets them entirely apart from machine-made goods. This value depends, not upon the fact that the article is made entirely by hand or with appropriate tools,—that is not the point,—but upon the skill of the workman, his power to appreciate his own work sufficiently to give it the quality that appeals to the cultivated taste and the care that he gives to every detail of workmanship, from the preparation of the raw material to the final finish of the piece. We are not urging that handicrafts be cultivated in connection with farming for the purpose of competing with the factories for the same class of trade, for, with the demand that necessitates the immense production of goods of all kinds, the labor-saving machinery and efficient methods of the factories are absolutely essential, just as they are essential in the general economic scheme because they furnish employment to thousands of workers who ask nothing better than to be allowed to tend a machine with a certainty of so much a day coming to them at the end of the week. The place of home and village industries on the economic side, is to supplement the factories by producing a grade of goods which it is impossible to duplicate by machinery,—and which command a ready market when they can be found,—and to give to the better class of workers a chance not only to develop what individual ability they may possess, but to reap the direct reward of their own energy and industry in the feeling that they are free of the wage system with all its uncertainties and that what they make goes to maintain a home that is their own, to educate their children and to lay up a sufficient provision against old age.

We do not deny that handicrafts, as practiced by individual arts and crafts workers in studios, fall very short of affording a sufficient living to craft workers as a class, and also we do not deny that small farming as carried on in our thinly populated districts is neither interesting, pleasant, nor profitable. But we do assert that it is possible to connect the two and to carry them on upon a basis that will insure not only peace and comfort in living, and a form of industry that affords the greatest opportunity for all-round development, but also a permanent competence. To bring about such a condition is the end and aim of the whole Craftsman idea. We call it by that name because we have been the first to formulate it in this country. But it is in the air everywhere. It is taking shape in several of the European countries in the form of government appropriations for the reëstablishment and encouragement of handicrafts among the people, government schools for the teaching of various crafts, and government exchanges to look after the question of a steady market. In Great Britain and Ireland the same thing is being done by private enterprise, partly as a matter of social reform and partly as an effort of philanthropy. But in this country conditions are different. We have no peasant class and almost the only people in need of social reform, or of philanthropic efforts in their behalf are the vast hordes of immigrants who pour into the country each year and too often find it difficult to adjust their lives to American conditions.

THE people to whom the Craftsman idea makes its appeal are the better class farmers who own their farms, workers in the city who are able to get together a little place in the country and build up a permanent home, and the better class of artisans who desire to escape from the routine of factory work. That such people are taking a keen interest in the question of life in the country and that farming is rapidly being restored to its former status as a desirable occupation is evidenced by the encouragement given to the widespread activities of the Department of Agriculture, which is doing so much to bring about better and more economical methods of cultivating the soil. We have plenty of proof that these efforts do not fall short in the matter of results, for all over the country there is a growing appreciation of the possibilities that lie in intensive agriculture and a desire to learn something of modern scientific farming. We most heartily endorse all that is being done along these lines; but we go a step farther because we maintain that the whole standard of living must be changed before there can be a return of natural conditions to our lives. For example, we have been accustomed of late years to an artificial scale of income and expenditure, and the prices of the most ordinary necessities of life have risen so high that it takes all the average man can do to make ends meet. This is both wrong and unnecessary, but a natural consequence of artificial conditions, and we maintain that the only way to correct it is to put ourselves in a position to realize that, in permitting our lives to be ruled by false standards and inflated values, we have lost sight of the principle that economy means wealth. When we regain this simple and reasonable point of view, we will find no difficulty in admitting that comfort and happiness in living do not depend upon the amount of money we can make and spend, but upon pleasant surroundings and freedom from the pressure of want and apprehension; and when this truth is brought home to the affairs of daily life, the work of establishing natural standards is done.

Therefore we advocate a return to cultivating the soil as a means of obtaining the actual living,—that is, of looking to garden, grain-patch, orchard, chicken yard and pasture for the vegetables, fruits, cereals, eggs and meat consumed by the family. If properly cared for and cultivated according to the modern methods that are now everybody's for the learning, a little farm of five or ten acres can be made not only to yield a living for its owner and his family but a handsome surplus for the markets, thus serving the double purpose of stopping the outflow and adding to the income of actual money as well as providing home comfort and healthful working surroundings. The farm home once established, its owner is free of any steady expense save for taxes and repairs, so that everything that is done is constructive and cumulative in its effects.

This, in brief, is the whole idea of the Craftsman home,—a pleasant comfortable dwelling situated on a piece of ground large enough to yield, under proper cultivation, a great part of the food supply for the family. Such a home, by its very nature, would be permanent and, with the right kind of education and healthful occupation for the children, would do much to stop the flow of population into the great commercial centers and to insure a more even division of prosperity throughout the land. In many instances the home is an established fact, but the education and the occupation are yet to come. It is with a view to solving this problem that we advocate individual handicrafts in the home and industries to be carried on upon a more extended scale in the neighborhood or the village. The very fact of a thorough training in any useful craft would insure to a boy or girl the right groundwork for an education, so that the solution of one problem is practically a solution of both.

Naturally, the greatest field for home handicrafts lies in the making of household furnishings, wearing apparel and articles of daily use. For example, there is a large and steady demand for hand-woven, hooked and hand-tufted rugs in good designs and harmonious colorings, especially when they can be had at reasonable prices. That there would be a market for good hand-made rugs in this country is shown by the demand for similar rugs that are made abroad by peasant labor. This is, of course, much cheaper than any class of labor in this country. Nevertheless, the same grade of rugs could be made here by home and farm workers and sold at a profit at the same price that must be demanded for the imported rugs, after the high import duty on this class of goods has been added to the original cost. Also cabinetmaking, considered as a handicraft, opens a field of unusually wide and varied interest, as the making of things so closely associated with our daily life and surroundings is a form of work that is both delightful and profitable. Iron work is equally interesting, and a preliminary training in good hard blacksmithing not only offers an excellent foundation for the doing of good things in structural iron work and articles for household use, but it equals wood work in developing any creative power that may be latent in the worker. Weaving and needlework come into the first rank of interesting and profitable crafts, and among the lighter industries that offer a chance for individual expression and at the same time pay pretty well, are basketry, block printing, dyeing, lace making, bookbinding and the like.

EVER since its first publication in nineteen hundred and one, THE CRAFTSMAN Magazine has, in one form or another, been advocating this idea; and we have most satisfactory proof in the growth and standing of the magazine that a great many people in this country are thinking along the same lines. When THE CRAFTSMAN was founded it was with the intention of making it a magazine devoted almost solely to the encouragement of handicrafts in this

THE CRAFTSMAN IDEA

country. We believed, then, as we believe now, in the immense influence for good in the development of character that is exerted merely by learning to use the hands. One needs only to look at any part of the history of handicrafts to realize how much strength, sincerity and genuine creative thought went into the work of the old craftsmen who were also such solid and substantial citizens. We have always felt that it is not the making of things that is important, but the making of strong men and women through the agency of the sound development that begins when the child learns to use its hands for shaping to the best of its ability something which is really needed either for its own play or for the comfort and convenience of others in the home. It is going back in spirit to the primitive beginning of handicrafts,—which marks the beginning of civilization, and is so important a factor in the growth of character that upon it depends nearly every quality of heart and brain that goes into what we may call the craftsmanship of life. But, as THE CRAFTSMAN grew and step by step attained a wider outlook, the question of the study of handicrafts as an end in itself gradually sunk to a position of minor importance in the policy of the magazine. Our belief that in it lay the foundation of all growth was no less, but the field was so broad that the record and discussion of all constructive work in the larger affairs of life came gradually to take first place.

As we began to design houses and to shape the idea of the Craftsman country home as we have here tried to describe it, we took up the subjects of architecture and interior decoration, doing our best to promote the establishment of the right standards and to offer all the aid in our power toward the development of a national spirit in our architecture. This naturally led to other forms of art, and THE CRAFTSMAN became a magazine for painters and sculptors as well as for architects, interior decorators and craftsmen. Along these lines it has always been progressive and rather radical, aiming always to discover and bring to the front any notable achievement that seemed to indicate the blazing of a new trail. The magazine has also taken the deepest interest in all social, industrial and political reforms and in the question of industrial education along practical lines that would fit any boy or girl to earn a living under any and all circumstances. In fact, taken altogether, THE CRAFTSMAN has been the outward and visible expression of the more philosophic side of the Craftsman idea, just as the houses and their furnishings have put into form its more concrete phases.

We have also paid a good deal of attention to agriculture in THE CRAFTSMAN, taking it up along very general lines. But we have felt that this is a field which required much more exhaustive treatment than we are able to give it in the pages of a magazine of this character. So to meet this need, we are about to establish a second magazine that will be called "THE YEOMAN" and that will be devoted entirely to the interests of farming, the possibilities of life in rural communities and to the handicrafts that might profitably be carried on in connection with agriculture.

THE time has come, however, to test out all the principles we have been advocating and give them the most practical and comprehensive demonstration within our power. Therefore we are this year opening a country place, where everything we have said can be put to the test of practical experience.

THE CRAFTSMAN IDEA

This place is called "Craftsman Farms" and it serves as a most complete exposition of the Craftsman idea as a whole. "Craftsman Farms" is situated in the hill country of New Jersey, and our intention is to make it a summer home and school for students of farming and handicrafts. While grown people are welcome, the chief object of the school's existence is to provide an opportunity for the instruction of boys and girls whose parents desire for them a method of training that will enable them to earn a living in whatever circumstances they may happen to be placed. In other words, we purpose to teach them to work with their hands,—not to hoe, dig, plow, or chop wood in a mechanical way,— but to do the kind of constructive work which requires direct thought and which will train them to cope with all the practical problems of life. In fact, the plan of the school is not only a return to the old system of apprenticeship, where the student learned his trade by mastering its difficulties one by one under the guidance of a master craftsman, but it is apprenticeship on improved lines because, instead of working for the benefit of the master, the student acquires by working solely for the sake of his own thorough training and the development in himself not merely skill but initiative and self-reliance.

The instruction will be in the form of lectures and informal talks from the teachers, who will not only give in this way such theoretical knowledge as seems to be required but will answer all questions and respond to all suggestions, so that the student's brain is necessarily made alert by his being forced to take an active part in his own training. The method of instruction will be the same throughout, whether the subject be agriculture, landscape gardening, house building, designing, or any one of the handicrafts. In the latter, students will work side by side with experienced craftsmen, so that every lesson will be the solving of some problem and the doing of actual work according to the methods employed by the best workmen.

For example, every man, sooner or later, hopes or intends to build himself a home. Imagine what that home might be if, as a boy, he had been trained to have a practical working knowledge of drawing, of construction, of the quality and use of different woods, of finishing these woods so that their full value would be brought out and of laying out the grounds surrounding his house so that the most harmonious environment would be a matter of course. As the thing stands now, most men hire some one else to do this sort of thing, which practically amounts to hiring some one else to think for them in matters that most intimately concern their personal life and surroundings.

It is now being very generally acknowledged that our present methods of education fail to a serious degree in the vital work of educating boys and girls toward the larger business of life,—toward the understanding of how to do, and the ability to do, those things upon which our physical existence depends. It does not by any means follow that training along lines of practical work will confine the future activities of the boy to manual labor or to the necessity of doing things for himself. He may use his abilities in as many other directions as he can, but we believe that learning to do the actual work of daily life in the country gives him a kind of ability that may be applied to any form of work, mental or manual, with the best effect, and also that any one possessing it may at any time get back to first principles and start afresh. It has always seemed to us that

THE CRAFTSMAN IDEA

the great disintegrating force in our modern way of living lies in the system by which everything is done by rote,—and largely by machinery,—and where labor of all kinds is so specially divided that a man, whether he be workman or director, has very little chance to cope with problems outside of his own particular line of work. The great purpose in life and work is the development of character and it naturally follows that true development can come only by the training and use of all the faculties in coping with all the problems that may come up in the ordinary course of life.

In addition to the instruction given at "Craftsman Farms," the conditions of life there will be such as to carry out the same idea. The students, whether young or old, will be housed in small hamlets scattered about the neighborhood in places chosen on account of their fitness for the several things to be done. Each group of cottages will be under the care of a house mother and an instructor and the student will go from hamlet to hamlet until, at the end of the course, he is not only master of the trade he has chosen to learn but also has a general knowledge of related trades and of farming. For example, most of the cottages in which the students live will be designed and built with their active assistance, as the students will be invited to use their own brains and creative ability in designing houses and cottages that they would like to live in or that seem suited to the place. In doing this, of course, they will work directly with the corps of architects that has in charge the designing of the cottages, and in the actual building the students will be allowed to work side by side with experienced carpenters, stone masons, wood finishers, cabinetmakers, blacksmiths and coppersmiths, so that every lesson will be the doing of actual work in the way it is done by competent workmen.

Aside from the educational feature of this enterprise, one of the main objects in carrying it out along the lines indicated is to put to a practical test our favorite theory of a farming community grouped around a central settlement where all social interchange and recreation are as full and convenient as they would be in the city and where every house is within easy reach of the farm lands that belong to it.

If the experiment should prove a success, we confidently look to see it put into practice by many other people; and if it should not, at least we shall have discovered its weak points and have learned something by experience. In any case, the school is meant to complete the work begun by the magazine and to give to the world the result of all the experience we have gained since the first inception of the Craftsman idea ten years ago. If it should have ever so little influence in bringing about the development of our national life along the lines laid down by the men who founded the Republic, it will have fulfilled its mission, because a truth which one man finds courage to utter today is echoed and applied by thousands tomorrow.